Indigenous Identity, Human Rights, and the Environment in Myanmar

This book draws on the experiences of the indigenous moveme.. Myanmar to explore how the local construction of indigenous identities connects communities to global mechanisms for addressing human rights and environmental issues.

Various communities in Myanmar have increasingly adapted international discourses of indigenous identity as a vehicle to access international legal mechanisms to address their human rights and environmental grievances against the Myanmar state. Such exercise of global discourses overlays historical endemic struggles of diverse peoples involving intersectional issues of self-determination, cultural survival, and control over natural resources. This book draws implications for the intersectionality of local and global theoretical discourses of indigeneity, human rights, and environment. It uses such implications to identify attendant issues for the aspirations of international human rights and environmental efforts and the practice of their associated international legal mechanisms. This book informs readers of the agency and capabilities of communities in underdeveloped countries to engage different global mechanisms to address local grievances against their states. Readers will develop a more critical understanding of the issues posed by the local construction of indigeneity for the ideals and practice of international efforts regarding human rights and the environment.

This book will be of great interest to students and scholars of indigenous studies, human rights, international law, Asian studies, development studies, and the environment.

Jonathan Liljeblad is Associate Professor at the Australian National University College of Law. He is the co-editor of *Indigenous Perspectives on Sacred Natural Sites* (Routledge, 2019) and co-editor of *Food Systems Governance* (Routledge, 2016). Born under the name Nanda Zaw Win, he is a member of the Pa-Oh indigenous peoples of Shan State, Myanmar.

Routledge Focus on Environment and Sustainability

The Sustainable Manifesto
A Commitment to Individual, Economical, and Political Change
Kersten Reich

Phyto and Microbial Remediation of Heavy Metals and Radionuclides in the Environment
An Eco-Friendly Solution for Detoxifying Soils
Rym Salah-Tazdaït and Djaber Tazdaït

Water Governance in Bolivia
Cochabamba since the Water War
Nasya Sara Razavi

Indigenous Identity, Human Rights, and the Environment in Myanmar
Local Engagement with Global Rights Discourses
Jonathan Liljeblad

Participatory Design and Social Transformation
Images and Narratives of Crisis and Change
John A. Bruce

Collaborating for Climate Equity
Researcher-Practitioner Partnerships in the Americas
Edited by Vivek Shandas and Dana Hellman

For more information about this series, please visit: www.routledge.com/Routledge-Focus-on-Environment-and-Sustainability/book-series/RFES

Indigenous Identity, Human Rights, and the Environment in Myanmar

Local Engagement with Global Rights Discourses

Jonathan Liljeblad

Routledge
Taylor & Francis Group

LONDON AND NEW YORK

First published 2022
by Routledge
4 Park Square, Milton Park, Abingdon, Oxon OX14 4RN

and by Routledge
605 Third Avenue, New York, NY 10158

Routledge is an imprint of the Taylor & Francis Group, an informa business

© 2022 Jonathan Liljeblad

The right of Jonathan Liljeblad to be identified as author of this work has been asserted in accordance with sections 77 and 78 of the Copyright, Designs and Patents Act 1988.

All rights reserved. No part of this book may be reprinted or reproduced or utilised in any form or by any electronic, mechanical, or other means, now known or hereafter invented, including photocopying and recording, or in any information storage or retrieval system, without permission in writing from the publishers.

Trademark notice: Product or corporate names may be trademarks or registered trademarks, and are used only for identification and explanation without intent to infringe.

British Library Cataloguing-in-Publication Data
A catalogue record for this book is available from the British Library

Library of Congress Cataloging-in-Publication Data
Names: Liljeblad, Jonathan, author.
Title: Indigenous identity, human rights and the environment in Myanmar : local engagement with global rights discourses / Jonathan Liljeblad.
Description: Abingdon, Oxon ; New York, NY : Routledge, 2023. |
Series: Routledge focus on environment and sustainability |
Includes bibliographical references and index.
Subjects: LCSH: Indigenous peoples–Burma–Social conditions. |
Indigenous peoples–Burma–Ethnic identity. | Indigenous
peoples–Burma–Civil rights. | Burma–Environmental conditions. |
Burma–Politics and government.
Classification: LCC GN635.B93 L55 2023 (print) |
LCC GN635.B93 (ebook) | DDC 305.8009591–dc23/eng/20220422
LC record available at https://lccn.loc.gov/2022007415
LC ebook record available at https://lccn.loc.gov/2022007416

ISBN: 978-0-367-67992-7 (hbk)
ISBN: 978-0-367-67994-1 (pbk)
ISBN: 978-1-00-313372-8 (ebk)

DOI: 10.4324/9781003133728

Typeset in Times New Roman
by Newgen Publishing UK

Contents

1 Introduction

Research Design and Methodology

In July 2015, an alliance of indigenous civil society organizations (CSOs) in Myanmar announced the formation of the Coalition of Indigenous Peoples in Myanmar/Burma (CIPM) for the dedicated purpose of making an inaugural submission of a report to the Universal Periodic Review (UPR) session on Myanmar (Snaing 2015). A mechanism of the United Nations (UN) Human Rights Council (HRC), the UPR, evaluates the human rights record of UN member states on a cyclical basis repeating approximately every five years (OHCHR 2021a). As a result, CIPM's action marked an attempt by Myanmar indigenous peoples to use an international human rights mechanism to address their concerns regarding the Myanmar state. The 2015 effort was not an isolated event, since CIPM continued to submit another report in the next UPR cycle of review for Myanmar in 2021 (HRC 2021a; HRC 2015).

During the same time period, Myanmar indigenous CSOs were also involved with the UN Framework Convention on Climate Change (UNFCCC), working through sympathetic international partners such as the Asia Indigenous Peoples Pact (AIPP) to engage different venues in the UNFCCC system on indigenous issues (AIPP 2021; AIPP 2020; AIPP 2015). While associated with the topic of climate change, the UNFCCC serves as an umbrella encompassing a range of related environmental issues and is open to indigenous peoples' perspectives (see, for example, UNFCCC REDD+ 2021a; IIPFCC 2021; LCIPP 2019a; UNFCCC 2019a). Similar to the case of the UPR, Myanmar indigenous CSOs engaged with UNFCCC mechanisms to address grievances against the Myanmar state (Myint 2017).

Conceptually, the activities of Myanmar indigenous CSOs for both the UPR and UNFCCC represented strategies to circumvent problems with the Myanmar state through appeal to global-level mechanisms, essentially dealing with local problems through recourse to institutions

DOI: 10.4324/9781003133728-1

and rules of international law. In such instance, "local" or "domestic" relates to sub-state spaces with actors and activities under the authority of a state that contrasts with "international" inter-state and supra-state spaces hosting actors and activities that work "transnationally" across state borders, "regionally" within an area of multiple states, or "globally" across the world. In doing so, Myanmar indigenous peoples demonstrated abilities to phrase their concerns and advance their interests in ways conforming to the practices of international human rights and international environmental discourses.

However, while both cases may be conceptually straightforward, the present analysis argues that they involve deeper workings with more complex dynamics that pose implications for understanding the agency of indigenous peoples in international spaces. The analysis investigates both scenarios, with the following chapters in this book exploring the challenges faced by Myanmar indigenous CSOs in engaging the UPR and UNFCCC and the attendant strategies they employed to overcome those challenges. In detailing such efforts, the chapters identify the nuances of agency across discourses on indigeneity, human rights, and environment, identifying the significance of Myanmar indigenous activities for conceptualizations of indigenous involvement in international affairs.

The sections below serve as an introduction to the analyses of the chapters in this book. Each section, respectively, presents the major themes driving the study, the specific directions of investigation undertaken in the disparate chapters, the broader aspects of the research method, and the outline of the next elements in this book. The next section provides a brief background on the history of global indigenous movements, which leads into a narrower review of scholarship focused specifically on the topic of "bottom-up" perspectives that focus on the efforts of indigenous groups to address local issues by reaching out to the international community for assistance. The analysis places the present assembly of chapters within the aforementioned literature, setting the purpose toward the Myanmar indigenous struggles to resolve grievances against the Myanmar state through strategies of engagement with international mechanisms. In doing so, Myanmar indigenous activists connect transnationally to international discourses of indigeneity, human rights, and environment. The discussion places such a research topic in relation to theoretical perspectives associated with studies on indigenous exercise of international institutions and rules. The analysis then summarizes the broader aspects of research method shared across the chapters in this book and finishes with an outline of the case study in each chapter in relation to the steps in analysis.

Global indigenous movements

The notion of global indigenous movements refers to activities between indigenous communities to build linkages, where linkages that cross nation-state borders are transnational and to the extent they seek associations irrespective of state sovereignty are international. While defined in relation to the presence of nation-states, the ideas of global indigenous movements encompass conceptualizations that differentiate the existence of indigenous peoples as distinct from nation-states. Such "Fourth World" approaches emphasize indigenous societies as opposed to the state-centric Cold War-era models tied to categories of a capitalist First World, socialist or Communist Second World, and underdeveloped Third World (Fukurai 2018; Alfred & Corntassel 2005; LaDuke 1983). In critiquing the prevailing state-based international system, Fourth World perspectives assert the existence of cultures with identifiable histories and traditions (Watson 2018; Alfred & Corntassel 2005; Griggs 1992; Manuel & Posluns 1974). Considerations of history and tradition reflect the arguments of literature that look to pre-colonial interactions between communities across geographies now divided by borders (see, for example, Koot 2020; Alfred & Corntassel 2005; Coates 2004; Hodgson 2002a, 2002b). Matching the attention to pre-colonial eras are studies of indigenous peoples within the colonies of European empires, whose expansion extended imperial powers across swaths of cultures spanning diverse continents (see, for example, Nettelbeck 2019; Sium et al. 2012; Anghie 2004; 2006; Alfred 2005; Coates 2004). The implications of historical review extend to current global interactions, with the potential for indigenous peoples to become international actors in politics and law (Watson 2018; Beier 2009; Beier 2007). In asserting a presence in the international realm, indigenous peoples operate within and without the state-centric system in the sense of holding identity distinct from the idea of nation-state that arose from the Peace of Westphalia 1648 which enshrined European experiences of sovereignty (Bruyneel 2007; Alfred 2005; Anghie 2004; 2006).

The assertion of indigenous concerns, to the extent that they serve cultural identity, align with notions of indigenous "nations" relative to states (Fukurai 2019; Alfred & Corntassel 2005; Niezen 2003). In essence, discourses on indigeneity delink notions of nation and state, with "nation" connoting cultural identity and "state" being political authority that arose in the era of European empires (Fukurai 2020; Fukurai 2019). The modern notion of nation-state traces to the Peace of Westphalia 1648, which brought the conception of sovereignty as tied to a state commanding loyalty of a nation (Farr 2005). The prevailing

Westphalian international system maintains the association of the two as nation-state, holding sovereignty that echoes colonial practices of dominion in terms of supreme authority over subject territories and peoples (Bruyneel 2007; Anghie 2004; 2006). State sovereignty differs from indigenous conceptions that involve more integral relations among diverse peoples with the surrounding natural world (Lightfoot 2016; Alfred 2005). Such differences in perspective result in divergent expectations of power, with the Westphalian system looking to issues of sovereignty and indigenous peoples tending to focus on concerns over self-determination (Bruyneel 2007; Lindroth 2006). Self-determination focuses on peoples rather than states and refers to the right of peoples to decide their own political status and development (Cambou 2019; Aguon 2010; UNDRIP 2007: Arts. 3–4). The scope of self-determination extends to indigenous issues impacted by international law (Charters 2010). However, indigenous notions of self-determination are nuanced, with disparate indigenous movements holding different aspirations that include building more equitable indigenous-state relations (Turner 2006); turning away altogether from the existing state-centric system, effectively seeking a new international order (Watson 2018; Coulthard 2014); or doing a mixture that combines autonomous governance and participatory engagement with states (Anaya 2009).

Despite the differences across indigenous peoples, there has been growth toward international solidarity, with an acceleration through the Cold War and post-Cold War eras (Poyer 2017; Powless 2012; Hall & Fenelon 2009; Niezen 2003). While arising in the wake of World War II, both eras incurred an expansion of international institutions and rules with a parallel increase in transnational movement of people, trade, and information. Such processes opened opportunities for more international interactions between peoples outside of sovereign state relations. Within such trends was the growth of transnational networks of indigenous activism that sought to build alliances across disparate indigenous cultures (see, for example, Krovel 2018; Lightfoot 2016; Escarcega 2012; Escarcega 2010; Hall & Fenelon 2009; Niezen 2009; Escobar 2008; Henderson 2008; Niezen 2003). The efforts in trans-national network formation have sought to accommodate the diversity of indigenous peoples while also identifying common interests, with a central concern being an assertion of self-determination (Lightfoot 2016; Niezen 2003; Muehlebach 2001). The mobilization of transnational networks reflects agency by indigenous peoples against the structure of an international system tied to states holding sovereignty in the form of exclusive jurisdiction of populations, territories, and resources within political boundaries (Rodriguez-Garavito 2011; Niezen 2003). The resulting growth of international indigenous activism is accompanied by a growth of indigenous identity, with diverse peoples seeking expression of their respective sensibilities within current global discourses even as they work to articulate them through existing international law (see, for example, Khan 2019; Puig 2019; Sloan 2013; Levi & Maybury-Lewis 2012; Wilson & Steward 2008; Jorgensen 2007; Lenzerini 2006). The underlying theme is one of self-empowerment, with indigenous peoples coalescing into a movement to contest state sovereignty on a global scale.

The apparent tension between global indigenous movements and a state-centric international system has not necessarily required that one come at the expense of the other. In particular, there have been trends to increase indigenous participation in the existing international order, going so far as to promote indigenous interests in the institutions and rules of global regimes such as the UN (Xanthaki 2014; Dahl 2012; Morgan 2007; Lindroth 2006; Kingsbury 1998). Institutions encompass bodies that convene and host discussions of diverse parties to address mutual concerns, such that they serve as fora enabling participation of stakeholders on shared issues. Rules relate to standards of conduct and arise as legal obligations or normative aspirations proscribing behavior, with manifestation in unwritten customs or written instruments. With respect to the UN, examples of institutional scope include the multi-decade thematic efforts that commenced with the 1993 International Year of the World's Indigenous Peoples, continued with the 1994 International Decade of the World's Indigenous Peoples, and extended further with the 2005 Second International Decade of the World's Indigenous Peoples. Collectively, they sought to promote the protection of indigenous cultures through greater indigenous rights; inclusion in policies; culturally appropriate development programs, monitoring and accountability; and funding to improve indigenous welfare (UN 2021a). Another institutional example is the 2014 World Conference on Indigenous Peoples, which was hosted by the UN with the purpose of identifying best practices to ensure indigenous rights (UN 2021a). In addition, in 2000, the UN established the Permanent Forum on Indigenous Issues (UNPFII) to enable a presence for indigenous voices within UN Economic and Social Council (UN 2021b; Lindroth 2006) and in 2001 created the post of Special Rapporteur on the Rights of Indigenous Peoples with a mandate to report on the situations of indigenous peoples in countries, advance standards and practices of indigenous rights, and investigate cases of rights violations (UN 2021c). Further spaces continue to appear in specialized UN agencies, as exemplified by the formation of the Indigenous Peoples' Forum in 2009 by the International Fund for Agricultural Development (IFAD 2021). On a higher level, the UN System Chief Executive Board for Coordination (UNSCEB) announced a Call for Action to support more indigenous participation in UN procedures, encourage country implementation of indigenous rights, advance increased accountability, and improve data collection on the status of indigenous peoples (UNSCEB 2021).

Of particular note has been the development of fora within thematic UN institutions for human rights and environment. With respect to the UN human rights system, from 1982 to 2007, the Working Group on Indigenous Populations (WGIP) served to render expertise to the Sub-Commission on the Promotion and Protection of Human Rights (UN 2021a). In 2007, the WGIP was superseded by the Expert Mechanism on the Rights of Indigenous Peoples (EMRIP), which exists as an advisory body on indigenous issues reporting directly to the HRC (EMRIP 2021). With respect to environment, in 2020, the UNFCCC launched a Local Communities and Indigenous Peoples Platform (LCIPP) with a dedicated Facilitative Working Group (FWG) and a purpose of sharing indigenous knowledge, improving indigenous capacity to engage with the UNFCCC, and integrating indigenous perspectives into climate change policies (LCIPP 2021; LCIPP 2019a). Similarly, the Convention on Biological Diversity (CBD) hosts the International Indigenous Forum on Biodiversity (IIFB), which began in 1996 with the goal of encouraging indigenous participation in the treaty (IIFB 2012).

With respect to rules, attendant with the trends for institutions furthering greater recognition and inclusion of indigenous peoples have been movements toward greater articulation of indigenous rights in international law (Dunbar-Ortiz et al. 2015; Phillips 2015; Xanthaki 2014; Powless 2012; Castellino 2010; Macklem 2008; Anaya 2004a; Kingsbury 1998). In particular, indigenous rights are explicitly listed in the International Labor Organization Convention 169 (ILO No. 169) of 1989 (ILO No. 169 1989) and the UN Declaration on the Rights of Indigenous Peoples (UNDRIP) of 2007 (UNDRIP 2007). Both instruments have limitations: as a declaration UNDRIP is non-binding, and while ILO No. 169 is a treaty with binding obligations on state parties it has only 24 ratifying members (Lenzerini 2019; Ormaza 2012; UNDRIP 2007; ILO No. 169 1989). Despite such issues, both serve a normative purpose of setting standards for states regarding the appropriate treatment of indigenous peoples.

Beyond ILO No. 169 and UNDRIP, indigenous rights are also addressed within other instruments focused on non-indigenous themes (Garcia & Lixinski 2020; Wardana 2012; Xanthaki 2009; Fodella 2006). For example, the Framework Principles on Human Rights and

Environment 2018 state in Principle 15 that "States should ensure that they comply with their obligations to indigenous peoples" by recognizing and protecting their rights to land and resources; gaining free, prior, and informed consent for actions affecting them; respecting their traditional knowledge and practices; and providing fair and equitable shares of benefits from activities on their lands and resources (HRC 2018a). Prior to such declaration, the UN Conference on Environment and Development (UNCED) 1992 asserted its Principle 22 that "Indigenous people and their communities ... have a vital role in environmental management and development" such that "States should recognize and duly support their identity, culture, and interests and enable their effective participation in ... sustainable development" (UNCED 1992: Principle 22). Similarly, the CBD (1992: Art. 8(j)) calls upon state parties to "respect, preserve, and maintain knowledge, innovations, and practices of indigenous and local communities ...". Accompanying the CBD is the Nagoya Protocol 2010, which provides provisions regarding access and benefits-sharing for traditional knowledge (Teran 2016; Nagoya Protocol 2010).

Apart from the aforementioned international environmental law, indigenous rights also arise within international human rights (Wardana 2012; Xanthaki 2009). Specifically, comparable to UNDRIP, both the International Covenant on Civil and Political Rights (ICCPR 1966) and the International Covenant on Economic, Social, and Cultural Rights (ICESCR 1966) provide the right of self-determination sought by indigenous movements (Chen 2017; ICCPR 1966: Art. 1; ICESCR 1966: Art. 1). Similarly, international human rights treaties encompass indigenous peoples due to their status as human beings (Corntassel & Primeau 2006). Of special relevance to indigenous identity is the right to culture contained in ICCPR Article 27, which protects the rights of minorities, either as individuals or groups "to enjoy their own culture, to profess and practise their own religion, or to use their own language" (ICCPR 1966: Art. 27). In addition, international human rights law works against potential discrimination impacting indigenous peoples, with General Recommendation 23 for the International Convention on the Elimination of All Forms of Racial Discrimination (ICERD) 1966 stating that indigenous peoples are protected by the convention and state parties are expected to recognize and respect indigenous culture; ensure the freedom and equality of indigenous peoples; provide indigenous peoples conditions for sustainable development compatible with their cultures; protect the effective participation of indigenous peoples in public life and guarantee informed consent to decisions affecting their rights and interests; ensure indigenous communities can exercise their rights to culture and language; and protect rights of indigenous peoples to own and control their lands and resources (CERD 1997).

Indigenous exercise of global mechanisms

Within the literature on global indigenous movements is scholarship focused on indigenous experiences to engage the expanding array of international institutions and rules. Described by terms such as "bottom-up," "grass-roots," or "from below," such scholarship looks to the perspective of indigenous activism across nation-state borders, with disparate studies exploring the struggles of particular individuals or groups addressing problems in their immediate surroundings by reaching out to global mechanisms in the form of institutions and rules in the international arena. The goals and strategies in using global mechanisms cover a diverse range, with the concept of bottom-up approaches reflecting a spectrum between those that lie more at the level of global mechanisms and those that are closer to the viewpoints of local communities. With respect to indigenous activities within global mechanisms, examples include Jens Dahl, who details how diverse indigenous groups began to engage the UN in the 1970s and over time formed a coalition that used the UN as a platform to advance a coherent agenda, such that they went beyond mere presence in UN spaces to alter the UN system itself (Dahl 2012). In addition, Rhiannon Morgan observes that indigenous involvement in the UN avoided potential moderation or homogenization of indigenous activism into the UN's prevailing institutional culture and so indicates the potential for indigenous activists to use global non-indigenous systems for resources and opportunities in support of indigenous interests (Morgan 2007). Further, James Anaya highlights the work of indigenous voices to expanding the space of indigenous rights within the UN system, reaching across human rights and environmental discourses to produce indigenous rights in international law (Anaya 2004a; Anaya 2004b).

With respect to bottom-up approaches from the perspective of local communities, there are studies covering indigenous activism across regions as diverse as the Americas, Africa, Asia, and Europe. Within the Americas, examples include the scholarship of Suzanne Sawyer and Allen Gerlach, each of whom offers work on indigenous groups in Ecuador who countered the extractive industries of multinational enterprises (MNEs) by mobilizing support from sympathetic activist organizations outside the country and pursued the use of litigation in courts of the MNE home countries to halt their development projects (Sawyer 2004; Gerlach 2003). Similarly, Pamela Martin investigates the work of Ecuadorian indigenous peoples to build transnational networks and identifies how they influence global mechanisms to alter international norms in ways more consistent with local indigenous ones (Martin 2011; Martin 2003). Together, Pamela Martin and Franke Wilmer compared indigenous movements in Ecuador and Bolivia that elevated themselves from local to global levels using transnational networks to bridge domestic and international processes (Martin & Wilmer 2017; Wilmer & Martin 2008). Comparable work is done by Cesar Rodriguez-Garavito and Luis Carlos Arenas, who see indigenous groups in Colombia also exercising transnational strategies against the afflictions of MNEs originating outside Colombia (Rodriguez-Garavito & Arenas 2005). Likewise, Ana Carolina Alfinito Vieira and Sigrid Quack detail the strategies of local indigenous groups in Brazil to form transnational alliances that engaged the Roman Catholic Church and international non-governmental organizations (NGOs) to advance indigenous rights (Vieira & Quack 2016). The nature of agency is advanced by Marc Brightman, whose research in the Guianas identifies the ways in which indigenous peoples manipulate identity in association with the circumstances of relations with non-Amerindians (Brightman 2008). Virginia Tilley studies how transnational indigenous movements encouraged El Salvador to recognize indigenous communities but were then weakened by European Union and UNESCO programs that ironically sought to support them (Tilley 2002).

Bottom-up approaches also exist for cases in Africa (Hodgson 2002a). For example, Sidsel Saugestad highlights how global-local alliances between international NGOs and San peoples worked to influence of court deliberations over indigenous rights in Botswana (Saugestad 2011). Also focused on the San is the work of Renee Sylvain, who identifies the struggles between the complexities of their identity against essentialist notions of indigeneity held by international discourses (Sylvain 2002). Michaela Pelican and Junko Maruyama compare the experiences of the San with the Mbororo peoples, asserting that their respective struggles in Botswana and Cameroon indicate agency in formulating creative strategies to tailor the global indigenous movement in ways more relevant for their specific concerns (Pelican & Maruyama 2015). In contrast, Dorothy Hodgson's work on indigenous movements in Africa, particularly with pastoralist groups such as the Maasai and Barabaig peoples, reveals the challenges of forming alliances across indigenous groups under the pressures of transnational indigenous rights groups and their related international donors (Hodgson 2009; Hodgson 2002a; Hodgson 2002b).

For Asia, Virginius Xaxa investigates how indigenous movements in India engaged with UN discourses over indigenous rights to advance domestic legislation promoting traditional indigenous governance and natural resource rights (Xaxa 2016). Micah Morton, Ian Baird, and Prasit Leepreecha trace the connections between the indigenous rights movement in Thailand with global indigenous discourses, which reframed Thai political debates to increase awareness of the marginalized status of minorities (Morton & Baird 2019; Leepreecha 2019). In studying the Ainu peoples of Japan, Daisuke Minami argues that the linkage between local and global is not straightforward, with cultural context serving to support and impede domestic indigenous engagement with transnational indigenous activism (Minami 2018).

Beyond particular regions, other scholarship studies efforts to grow global movements. Maria Elena Martinez-Torres and Peter Rosset, for example, present La Via Campesina as a transnational peasant movement comprised of local organizations from the Americas, Europe, and Africa encompassing indigenous rights groups working to challenge international forces such as multinational corporations, World Trade Organization, and World Bank (Martinez-Torres & Rosset 2010).

The bottom-up approaches in the above literature illuminate a growing sophistication of indigenous peoples vis-à-vis international strategies to connect struggles in local contexts with global discourses, particularly via engagement in international institutions and rules (Hasenclever & Narr 2018; Lennox & Short 2016; Anaya 2004a; Anaya 2004b). The sophistication reflects indigenous responses to the challenges of using unfamiliar practices and concepts associated with global mechanisms, which can be understood as falling into categories of ontology regarding the approach to international institutions and rules; epistemology in relation to forms of understanding tied to use of such institutions and rules; and resourcing in terms of materials and financing to pursue activities involving those institutions and rules. Ontologically, the scholarship observes indigenous activists adapting global mechanisms across thematic areas, with cross-issue linkages between indigenous rights, human rights, and environment that use international human rights law to address indigenous concerns in environmental regimes and international environmental law to support indigenous concerns in human rights regimes (see, for example, Belfer et al. 2019; Pearl 2018; Mengden 2017; Noisecat 2016; Harry 2011; Anaya 2004b). Epistemologically, the literature identifies the difficulties posed by contrasting worldviews and knowledge systems, as indigenous actors from frequently subordinate positions in the Global South encounter international institutions and rules predicated on dominant paradigms of understanding and practice largely derived from cultures in the Global North (see, for example, Liljeblad & Verschuuren 2019; Gombay & Palomino-Schalscha 2018;

Escobar 2008). With respect to resourcing, the literature also identifies the challenges of indigenous groups from impoverished backgrounds in underdeveloped societies, which incurs a hurdle in terms of gaining the knowledge, skills, and financing needed to engage with the practices and concepts specific to given global mechanisms (see, for example, Belfer et al. 2019; Martin 2011; Rodriguez-Garavito & Arenas 2005).

In developing their sophistication vis-à-vis international institutions and rules, indigenous peoples have increased their capacities through a range of transnational strategies that fit within theories of social movements, intermediaries, and networks. At a base level, the coalescence of indigenous activists into organizations follows notions of social movement formation, with efforts at outreach to sympathetic international actors then aligning with literature on transnational social movements that center on the mobilization of peoples in different states for sustained campaigns seeking social or political change (Tilly & Tarrow 2015; della Porta & Tarrow 2004). While indigenous CSOs may arise at a local or domestic level in terms of the sub-state spaces under the jurisdiction of a state, they can escalate their activism by linking to broader social movements operating at international levels in terms of spanning multiple nation-states and amplifying issues into global discourses (see, for example, Morgan 2007; Martin 2003). Attendant with the efforts of local social movements to reach international actors are theories of transnational advocacy networks (TANs), which help to describe transnational strategies of activism as involving networks of actors working collectively across nation-states to advance shared values (Keck & Sikkink 1998). By connecting to actors associated with such networks, indigenous activists can raise local issue to global audiences and international mechanisms (see, for example, Liljeblad 2018; Sargent 2012; Rodriguez-Garavito & Arenas 2005). Further to conceptions of social movements and advocacy networks is the idea of intermediaries, who are actors occupying middle positions between local and global discourses, translating ideas and meanings into their respective vernacular (Merry 2006). Indigenous groups can use intermediaries to facilitate engagement with other actors operating in the international realm, with intermediaries effectively helping indigenous groups with limited capacities acquire the knowledge, skills, and resources necessary to participate with transnational partners and international institutions (see, for example, Lupien 2020; Claeys 2018; Eichler 2018; Sanmuki 2013).

The analysis in subsequent chapters of the present analysis demonstrates permutations of the above concepts in the experiences of Myanmar indigenous CSOs in connecting to international discourses regarding indigeneity, human rights, and environment. Chapter 2 addresses the nature of the indigenous movement in Myanmar, noting the rise of indigenous CSOs in association with international assistance and situating their work within the global ideas of indigeneity. Chapter 3 focuses on Myanmar indigenous use of the UN HRC's UPR mechanism, presenting its conceptual alignment with ideas of TANs but highlighting deeper complexities entailing a mixture of transnational strategies. In comparison to Chapter 3, Chapter 4 looks to Myanmar indigenous involvement with the UNFCCC, identifying its reflection of TANs but detailing the scale of intricacies associated with engagement in the diverse components of the UNFCCC system and the consequent implications for a broad exercise of different transnational strategies. Chapter 5 summarizes the collective findings and theoretical implications of the aforementioned chapters and then applies them to generate larger consequences for scholarship dealing with indigenous peoples in discourses connecting human rights and environment as well as indigenous, or Fourth World, perspectives in international law.

Directions for study

The cumulative literature on the growth of a global indigenous movement constitutes a rich body of material encompassing a broad range of topics receiving attention from an array of disciplines. Within the specific subfield of bottom-up indigenous engagement with global mechanisms, the scholarship provides deep analyses that inform theoretical conceptions of transnationalism and indigenous activism, with details in local–global connections adding to discourses in international relations and international law. The empirical works within the scholarship also provide insights for practice, featuring case studies that generate findings of potential use for other contexts. In highlighting the experiences of select indigenous groups, the case studies present lessons for other indigenous efforts seeking to employ international strategies.

Aspirations for more general application, however, should be undertaken with care. There are a number of factors that provide caution in utilizing the theoretical and practical findings from existing case studies to other indigenous struggles. To begin, indigenous experiences are not always consistent in that they vary across peoples under disparate circumstances. As much as historical efforts sought to build a global indigenous movement, they did so while contending with a plurality of worldviews, knowledge systems, histories, and struggles (Lightfoot 2016; Niezen 2003; Muehlebach 2001). There has been a measure of consensus in claiming a right to self-determination, but such a consensus is complicated by varying conceptions of self-determination (Chen 2017; Ivison 2006). The diversity of indigenous peoples renders their respective experiences context-specific and so poses a tension between conceptions of indigenous activism as converging to a monolithic global phenomenon versus an assembly of unique and possibly divergent communities. To the extent that there are common issues, the existing case studies in the literature offer the promise of broader utility; to the extent that there are differences, they raise the challenge of contextually limited application.

Beyond differences of experience are differences of identity, with the meanings of concepts related to indigeneity subject to diverse perspectives within both non-indigenous and indigenous discourses (Chen 2017). The differences over indigeneity exist at multiple levels, with ambiguity in discourses at international, regional, and state levels (Niezen 2003; Kingsbury 1998). Within Asia, for example, are competing perspectives over the meaning and composition of "indigenous" that stretch across multiple dimensions: (1) sub-state groups of peoples who exercise self-determination to set their own respective criteria for identifying themselves as indigenous; (2) states asserting their authority as sovereigns to prescribe definitions of what constitutes indigenous; and (3) a regional perspective that claims Asia as being unique, and hence exceptional, from international discourses (Kingsbury 1998). The divisions over the meaning of indigeneity intensify the tensions between universality and context specificity, furthering the uncertainty over the potential for existing case studies in the literature to provide more generalizable lessons.

Compounding the diversity in experience and identity is the uncertainty over cosmopolitan and nationalist aspects of indigenous status. Indigenous cosmopolitanism refers to a sensibility that transcends place, so that a distinctive group of indigenous people maintains translocal cohesion irrespective of geography (Forte 2010; Ivison 2006). In contrast, indigenous nationalism relates to self-determination in the sense of seeking integrity of culture and territory under self-government (Ivison 2006). Cosmopolitanism implies greater receptivity of transnational engagement with the gamut of political, legal, and cultural systems in the world; nationalism points to separation, not just from non-indigenous forces but extending even as far as other peoples who also claim to be indigenous (Mercado 2011; Forte 2010; Goodale 2006; Ivison 2006). Cosmopolitanism supports efforts to apply the experiences of one indigenous people to others, while nationalism question the relevance of generalizations.

The complexity posed by the above issues raise a question about the extent to which the existing literature on bottom-up perspectives of indigenous engagement with global mechanisms applies for all indigenous peoples. On one hand, the discourse over the global indigenous movement suggests that commonalities in experience, identity, and cosmopolitan outlook allow insights from an individual case to be useful for other contexts. On the other hand, the arguments regarding diversity raise the possibility of divergent experiences, identities, and nationalist sentiments that emphasize the specificities of context and discourage attempts to connect different cases. It is possible to resolve the apparent tension through an aggregation of case studies, which is an outcome of the growth in the literature summarized in preceding sections regarding indigenous movements and their engagement with international institutions and rules. The accumulation of case studies, however, means a continual addition of empirical work to expand the nuances in understanding implied by the complexities of context, identity, and cosmopolitanism reflected in indigenous activities at transnational outreach. Hence, there is space for exploration of indigenous movements, with additional research on additional cases helping to add further insights to the existing body of scholarship.

The present study follows the above call by contributing study of the efforts by Myanmar indigenous CSOs to engage international mechanisms to address their grievances against the Myanmar state. In particular, the analysis explores the strategies undertaken by Myanmar indigenous peoples to elevate domestic issues within Myanmar to the global spaces of the UPR process of the UN HRC and the UNFCCC. The analysis approaches Myanmar indigenous outreach to the UPR and UNFCCC as examples of "bottom-up" scenarios of indigenous movements reaching out to international institutions and rules. The situation of Myanmar, however, offers potential value for the existing scholarship in terms of (1) illuminating the intricacies associated with the introduction of the concept of indigeneity into preexisting identity discourses and (2) detailing the exercise of international mechanism as vehicles for cross-issue linkages and global strategies.

First, with respect to the concept of indigeneity, Myanmar represents a case of a country with a history of identity politics whose parameters have been tied to ideas of races, ethnicities, and nationalities. The adoption by Myanmar peoples to describe themselves represents a turn in identity discourse, with references to international definitions of indigeneity reflecting an effort to import international conceptualizations into a domestic space. The introduction of indigeneity into Myanmar's identity politics is not straightforward, in that the discussions of indigeneity in international instruments such as the UN Declaration on Rights of Indigenous Peoples (UNDRIP) encompass arguments for self-determination, which directly counters the interests of the Myanmar state to unify the country and pacify its myriad armed conflicts with a host of peoples seeking autonomy (Dittmer 2010; Taylor 2009; South 2008). As a result, Myanmar poses a challenge for the promotion of indigenous identity, with the country's continuing internal struggles with identity tied to fractious politics with perpetual civil wars (Dittmer 2010; Taylor 2009; South 2008), such that the introduction of international discussions of indigeneity asserting self-determination risk inserting a potentially destabilizing element exacerbating the fragility of the country. The analysis in the next chapters investigates the adoption of indigeneity by Myanmar peoples, exploring how and why identity groups drew upon conceptions of indigeneity, the connections between those conceptions with international ideas of indigeneity, and the place of Myanmar indigenous peoples within the larger global discourse on indigeneity.

Second, in exercising indigeneity consistent with international definitions of the idea, Myanmar indigenous groups were able to access international mechanisms. Specifically, the analysis in following chapters argues that Myanmar indigenous CSOs employed indigeneity as a vehicle to gain support that empowered them to engage the UPR and the UNFCCC. In doing so, the analysis asserts Myanmar indigenous efforts employed cross-issue linkages, framing indigenous interests for the environment as human rights issues under the purview of the UPR and indigenous interests regarding human rights as climate change issues fitting within the concerns of the UNFCCC. Moreover, the following chapters points out that engagement with global-level mechanisms such as the UPR and UNFCCC entailed exercise of broader transnational strategies involving a range of actors spanning domestic and international spaces, such that Myanmar indigenous activists displayed abilities to exercise systematic, coordinated campaigns employing diverse approaches that framed their local interests in ways amenable to international institutions and rules.

Following the above, Myanmar presents a unique scenario for "bottom-up" perspectives of indigenous engagement with global mechanisms, with Myanmar offering a case with indigeneity being an introduced concept to an unstable domestic politics that enabled peoples to rephrase local concerns in ways connecting to international assistance. The subsequent chapters explore the activities of Myanmar indigenous peoples with respect to the adoption of indigenous identity, use of the UPR, and exercise of the UNFCCC. Collectively, they work to add the experiences of Myanmar indigenous struggles to the existing case studies of indigenous movements in other locations, complementing their insights with the nuances of Myanmar's context.

Research methodology

The analysis of the following chapters uses case study approaches involving qualitative data drawn from fieldwork of Myanmar indigenous CSOs, and while the nature of research differs for each chapter, there are several common issues that should be noted with respect to positionality, bounding of scope regarding actors, bounding of scope regarding time, and the use of sources vis-à-vis the hazards of research in Myanmar. First, in keeping with the concerns of qualitative methods with marginal groups, the author presents a statement of positionality (see, for example, Shaw et al. 2019; Bourke 2014). The author identifies as an indigenous person from the Pa-Oh indigenous peoples of Shan State, Myanmar. While born in Shan State, the author grew up in the United States and received a Western education. The author is employed as a research scholar at an Australian university, with research and teaching expertise in international law and international relations. Because of such a dual background, the author was able to connect the divide between the worlds of Myanmar indigenous struggles with international perspectives. The position as a bicultural bridge between local and international discourses made the author an asset sufficient to serve as a consultant with several of the Myanmar indigenous CSOs included in the present study, with the author delivering capacity-building workshops on international law related to indigenous rights, human rights, and environmental issues.

In describing positionality, the author acknowledges potential biases arising from the application of non-indigenous perspectives on indigenous issues, including the division in worldviews between international discourses associated with indigenous rights, the UPR, and UNFCCC and local discourses of Myanmar peoples. The author works to mitigate bias by applying a bicultural background to maintain sensitivity of diverse viewpoints and concerns of the topics under study, respecting the need to protect the disadvantaged and vulnerable voices of marginalized peoples. In addition, the author also tries to reduce bias by triangulating data from different sources, with the goal of using them to identify divergent perspectives and discerning common observations. Further, in noting the position of capacity-building trainer, the author follows the guidance of indigenous scholarship calling for research built upon long-term researcher–community relationships with mutual capacity-building fulfilling de-colonial purposes of empowering indigenous peoples (Kovach 2021; Chilisa 2020; Jull et al. 2018; Goodman et al. 2017; Hart et al. 2017; Castleden et al. 2012; Ball & Janyst 2008; Smith 2007; Niezen 2003). The capacity-building sessions and fieldwork in the present study lasted during the years 2015–2020, during which time the researcher and the Myanmar indigenous CSOs in the analysis formed an ongoing relationship wherein the production of knowledge involved mutual learning of the divisions and connections between Myanmar indigenous worldviews and international law concepts, with the ulterior motive being increased capabilities of indigenous CSO members to apply principles of international law regarding human rights and the environment. Moreover, in keeping with the principles of transparent researcher–indigenous partnerships (Goodman et al. 2017; Hart et al. 2017; Ball & Janyst 2008), the Myanmar indigenous CSOs under study retained rights of reviewing and editing drafts of each chapter.

Second, the scope of study is bounded in terms of actors to Myanmar indigenous CSOs involved with the UPR and UNFCCC. With respect to the actors, some care should be observed in that there were differences in the organizations across the topics of the subsequent chapters. Specifically, Chapter 2 describes the interactions between Myanmar CSOs with the AIPP, a regional indigenous organization with a membership comprised of sub-state indigenous CSOs from various Asian countries, in the promotion of indigeneity in Myanmar and the formation of the Coalition of Indigenous Peoples Myanmar (CIPM). Chapter 3 observes that Myanmar indigenous engagement with the UPR was through the CIPM. In contrast, in Chapter 4's study of the UNFCCC, there was no role played by CIPM and Myanmar indigenous action occurred via the AIPP. Across all chapters, the slate of Myanmar indigenous CSOs is not consistent. The inconsistency, however, is countered by the focus of analysis, which is not directed at comparing the conduct of a single individual or cohort of Myanmar indigenous CSOs across different international mechanisms but rather on the dynamics exhibited generally by Myanmar indigenous CSOs involved with either the UPR or UNFCCC. As a result, the analysis in the following chapters is presenting differences in the strategies employed vis-à-vis global conceptions of indigeneity, UPR, and UNFCCC, such that the extent of a control is the condition of activity by any Myanmar indigenous CSOs for each respective discourse.

Third, the scope of study is also bounded in time to the period of fieldwork 2015–2020. During that time, Myanmar attempted a comprehensive transition encompassing political, economic, and social changes of greater liberalization supported by technical assistance, investment, and trade from a broad array of international aid organizations and foreign states (Fink 2014; Ganesan 2013; Callahan 2012; Englehart 2012). The scale of reform was reflected in new laws regarding infrastructure, human development, education, energy, and foreign investment; a broad peace process to end conflict with multiple ethnic armed organizations; programs to promote rule of law, human rights, and independence of the legal and judicial professions; projects for infrastructure and human development; and efforts for good governance (Fink 2014; Ganesan 2013; Callahan 2012; Englehart 2012; Hlaing 2012). The changes occurred under a process of democratization that sought to move from military to civilian rule (Fink 2014; Ganesan 2013; Callahan 2012; Englehart 2012). The breadth and pace of the attendant dynamics meant fluid conditions that challenged timely analysis. Because of such ephemeral circumstances, the study held to a longitudinal perspective that used the long-term researcher–subject relationships to constantly re-evaluate new data in alignment with the indigenous scholarship identified above.

The period 2015–2020 means a temporal scope that precedes the February 2021 military coup (*The Guardian* 2021a), and hence misses a significant alteration in the domestic Myanmar political space. The potential issue of timeliness, however, is alleviated by the purpose of the study, which is less about the interactions between Myanmar indigenous peoples and the Myanmar state and more about the efforts of Myanmar indigenous CSOs to use the UPR and UNFCCC. As much as their efforts were motivated by grievances against the state, those grievances were tied to ongoing issues that span civilian and military eras. Chapter 2, in particular, summarizes the history of Myanmar indigenous struggles, clarifying how the return of a military regime is likely to restore past intensities heightening motivations for international assistance from entities like the UPR and UNFCCC.

Last, the following chapters address topics of indigeneity, human rights, and environment that involve heightened sensitivities in Myanmar. Chapter 2 observes how indigenous rights, particularly in connection with international definitions encompassing rights of self-determination, exacerbate the tensions between the Myanmar state and the country's various minorities. Chapter 3 raises the chronic deficiencies of Myanmar on human rights. Chapter 4 similarly notes the country's weak protection of its environment. The slate of issues is compounded by the February 2021 military coup, which has resulted in an escalation of internal armed conflict against minorities, increased violations of human rights, and acceleration of environmental degradation (Bloomberg 2021; Engineering & Technology 2021; ICG 2021; PRIO 2021; *The Guardian* 2021b; UN News 2021; UNSC 2021).

The analysis seeks to mitigate the above dangers, employing whenever possible publicly accessible primary and secondary sources reflecting information already in circulation, with the purpose of avoiding further disclosure of sensitive data or identities. Primary sources involve documents from UN databases related to the UPR and UNFCCC, NGOs involved with both mechanisms, and Myanmar indigenous CSOs. Secondary sources consist of scholarly studies and news media relevant to the topics of indigenous peoples, the UPR, and UNFCCC. To the extent that the analysis draws on field notes and interviews collected during the period of fieldwork, the analysis removes information that might allow inference of identities, seeks editing by sources, and maintains confidentiality.

Steps in analysis

The following chapters reflect the steps in analysis. Chapter 2 addresses the concept of indigeneity in Myanmar, which is contested in terms of its application and in its meaning. The chapter presents an overview of the diverse perspectives on indigeneity manifested in scholarly discourses, their association with issues in international law, and the contrasting ideas expressed in different country contexts. The chapter then contrasts such discourses with the notion of indigeneity in Myanmar, noting the position of the Myanmar state on indigenous rights and the growth of indigenous identity among Myanmar's minorities. The analysis identifies the interactions between international actors and Myanmar minorities in formulating conceptions of indigenous identity that connect to international understandings of indigeneity.

Chapter 3 focuses on Myanmar indigenous outreach to the UPR mechanism of the UN HRC. The chapter highlights how the Myanmar indigenous CSOs overcame their lack of capacity to form a coalition with the knowledge, skills, and resources needed to participate in the UPR. The analysis explores the strategies they used vis-à-vis the UPR to address environmental grievances of indigenous peoples in Myanmar. Drawing upon their experiences, the analysis draws implications for theoretical understanding of Myanmar indigenous engagement with the UPR.

Chapter 4 follows the orientation of Chapter 3, investigating Myanmar indigenous participation in the UNFCCC. The chapter notes the issues faced by Myanmar indigenous CSOs in working through the UNFCCC system to address their human rights concerns. The discussion explores their strategies to overcome such issues and identifies the implications for theoretical conceptualizations of Myanmar indigenous involvement with the UNFCCC.

Chapter 5 draws broader implications for theory from the findings of the previous chapters. The chapter reviews the insights of previous chapters regarding Myanmar indigenous use of the UPR and UNFCCC to address their local concerns against the Myanmar state. The analysis asserts the significance of such efforts in understanding the nature of indigenous agency in the fields of international relations and international law. The chapter finishes by noting directions for additional research.

2 The Construction of Indigenous Identity in Myanmar

Local Adaptation of International Discourses of Indigeneity

In exploring the nature of Myanmar indigenous agency, it is helpful to provide an antecedent discussion regarding the notion of indigeneity to clarify the parameters of activism by Myanmar indigenous peoples. The present chapter does so by placing the concept of indigeneity in Myanmar in relation to international discourses. The following sections begin with a brief comment on theory and method specific to the present chapter. The analysis proceeds with a review of broader global discourses on indigeneity and the accompanying expression in international law. The discussion continues with a comparative review of cases from different geographic locations, with the goal of delineating the issues that were made apparent from claims to indigenous identity in diverse contexts. The analysis then turns to the manifestation of indigeneity in Myanmar, discussing its status under the Myanmar state and its use by Myanmar minorities. In doing so, the analysis identifies the connections between Myanmar identity politics and global discourses over the idea of indigeneity. This chapter finishes with conclusions that note the consequent implications for the analyses in the remainder of this book.

Theory and methodology

The purpose of placing Myanmar indigenous perspectives within larger global discourses entails delineation of the parameters in understanding across different viewpoints about the idea of indigeneity, which directs the bulk of present discussion toward a literature review of the conceptions of indigeneity circulating in international spaces and comparative contexts. In keeping with Chapter 1, "international" relates to inter-state and supra-state activities encompassing interactions among state and non-state actors across state borders and within international institutions exemplified by the Universal Periodic Review (UPR)

DOI: 10.4324/9781003133728-2

and UN Framework Convention on Climate Change (UNFCCC). Additionally, "comparative" refers to the contrast between activities occurring in spaces under the authority of individual states, where the space under a single state constitutes a "domestic" or "local" realm of actors whose conduct may differ from the conduct of actors in another domestic arena. As a consequence, the present analysis views indigeneity in Myanmar in terms of domestic civil society organizations (CSOs) adopting meanings of indigeneity which connect with aspects of various definitions expressed by international actors and international law and conforms to some trends displayed by indigenous movements in other locales outside Myanmar.

However, to the extent that Myanmar indigenous CSOs worked with sympathetic international actors in reaching out to broader discussions outside Myanmar, their dynamics evoke the theory of intermediaries. An element of norm diffusion scholarship, the idea of an intermediary denotes an actor that facilitates the communication of ideas and meanings between domestic and international discourses (Bettiza & Dionigi 2015; Golan & Orr 2012; Merry 2006). Intermediaries effectively hold a middle position, helping to convey information that enables engagement by local actors with global ones (Bettiza & Dionigi 2015; Golan & Orr 2012; Merry 2006). Because of their role in directing the flow of ideas and meanings, intermediaries have an ability to influence the outcomes of deliberations by local actors regarding international norms (Merry 2006).

Exploration of indigeneity in Myanmar, with respect to both larger global discourses and intermediaries, requires a brief note regarding method. Following the methodological issues addressed in Chapter 1, the following sections exercise precaution in referencing Myanmar indigenous CSOs. The analysis relies largely on preexisting publicly accessible primary and secondary sources compiled from scholarly literature; news media; and reports of government agencies, CSOs, nongovernmental organizations (NGOs), and international institutions. As much as the discussion draws on field notes and interviews from a particular Myanmar indigenous CSO, the analysis uses pseudonyms and minimizes their use to avoid data that may allow inference of organizational or individual identities.

Dimensions of discourse

The concept of indigeneity involves perception of a person or people as being indigenous (Bello-Bravo 2019; Merlan 2009). The concept, however, is subject to contestation, with a discourse hosting various perspectives in its meaning. The diversity of interpretations poses some ambiguity, with different approaches holding separate criteria that at times lead to opposing understandings (see, for example, Baird 2020; Timperley 2020; Bello-Bravo 2019; Gregg 2019; Merlan 2009). The variations in understanding are significant not just for abstract considerations of theory but also for the delineation of sociocultural issues and political-legal claims (Timperley 2020; Gregg 2019; Niezen 2009; Niezen 2003; Brown & Sant 1999). It is possible to clarify the complexities in the discourse by organizing the various perspectives in categories of debate in terms of issues that are relational, in the sense of indigeneity being identified relative to something else, or intrinsic, in the sense of having indigeneity being qualities possessed by a group or individual irrespective of other actors.

Relational facets of indigeneity

Relational arguments over indigeneity encompass political, organic, geographic, and temporal frameworks that place the status of being indigenous in connection with something else. First, with respect to politics, the discourse hosts arguments that interpret indigeneity as being in struggle against dominant forces. The dominant presence is often interpreted as being sovereign states in that indigenous peoples exist apposite to the encroachment of both a global state system and individual states. The common framework is one of colonialism and post-colonialism, wherein indigeneity involves the appellation of indigenous to peoples who were colonized by European empires, subordinated within European colonial administration, and continue to be marginalized in the post-independence states that supplanted expired European colonies. Within such a framework, the current global system is an extension of colonialism in that the current world continues an imperial hierarchy of inequality with hegemonic positions that suppress subaltern cultures and extract resources from subaltern communities (Alfred & Corntassel 2005; Anghie 2005). Indigenous peoples are among the subalterns and struggle to protect their cultures and communities from the corrosive impacts of exploitative global processes (Alfred & Corntassel 2005). Similarly, individual states also sustain a legacy of colonialism, with post-independence states maintaining structures of power inherited from colonial administrators that reified elites and subjugated marginalized populations (Bruyneel 2007; Alfred & Corntassel 2005). Indigenous peoples hold marginal positions under the authority of the state, laboring to protect themselves from political and legal institutions that circumscribe their rights and identities (Gregg 2019; Bruyneel 2007).

Apart from the struggle against states, political frameworks also encompass arguments that relate indigeneity in terms of subordination not to states but to other peoples. Such conceptions of indigeneity see marginalization that either existed prior to colonialism or continues to exist post-colonialism, such that the focus is on subaltern status in a hierarchy of groups. In such approaches, it is possible for different peoples to oppress each other separate from the state, with the state having the potential role of protecting subordinate groups (Barnard 1998). Within the hierarchy of society, indigeneity can be claimed by groups at subordinate levels suffering the afflictions from those in superior positions of power (see, for example, Wolf & Heidmann 2014; Merlan 2009; Baviskar 2007).

Second, going beyond political frameworks, relational concerns also arise with more organic considerations vis-à-vis connections to the environment. While still phrased in colonial and post-colonial terms, attention is to the underlying worldviews promoted by European imperial expansion, which entailed European experiences with sovereignty tied to notions of dominion that saw territories, populations, and natural world as resources available for consumption by those wielding authority (Bruyneel 2007; Alfred 2005; Anghie 2005). Against such worldviews, discourse asserts a contrast with alternative indigenous perspectives holding different perspectives of the relationship between humans and nature. A portion of indigenous studies literature asserts the existence of indigenous cultures that while consistent with notions of dominion deviated from Eurocentric power structures and instead used natural resources in accordance with different context-specific management systems (see, for example, Krech III 1999). Other scholarship goes further, arguing that indigenous cultures are more ecologically sensitive and exercise more holistic understanding of human–nature relationships with higher awareness of their interdependencies, more effort to promote equity between peoples and the environment, and more harmonious coexistence between them via more sustainable lifestyles (see, for example, Urzedo et al. 2021; Ormaza 2012; Powless 2012; Harkin & Lewis 2007).

Third, related to relationships with the environment are frameworks that discuss indigeneity in connection to geography, in the sense that debates over indigeneity consider the extent to which indigenous culture is tied to location (Clifford 2013). Location-specific perspectives see indigenous culture as developing in association with physical context and so connected to the features of its surrounding natural space. The implication is that an individual's identity as a member of an indigenous community can be lost once the person migrates, since relocation constitutes a disconnection from site specific to the community's culture (de la Cadena & Starn 2007). In contrast, more cosmopolitan perspectives posit that indigenous identity is not fixed to location but is a more internalized sensibility that may originate in a particular site but which travels with an individual to new physical spaces. As a result, identification as a member of a given indigenous culture can exist despite migrations involving rural–urban or cross-border transitions (Gregg 2019; Clifford 2013; Forte 2010).

Fourth, related to the preceding facets of indigeneity are temporal frameworks that include time in determining indigenous identity. Temporal considerations can be implicit or explicit in referencing time, with implicit associations involving indeterminate historical moments and explicit associations identifying specific historical moments. Implicit associations with time are exemplified by arguments that view indigeneity as involving the status of descent from peoples who were first to inhabit a location (Saugestad 2001). Explicit associations are exemplified by viewpoints that define indigeneity as tied to peoples who existed at the time of arrival of European colonizers (Eide 2009).

Intrinsic

Distinct from relational factors in conceptualizing indigeneity are approaches that address more inherent qualities disconnected from comparison to something else. Inherent, or intrinsic, attributes are reflected in debates over whether indigeneity is inalienable or alienable, static or dynamic, and culturally distinct or malleable. First, the opposition of inalienability versus alienability is reflected in the conflict between perspectives that see indigeneity as inalienable in the sense that it is not something people can choose but rather a quality inherent to their being, versus perspectives that view indigeneity as alienable in the sense of being something socialized and hence capable of being acquired or lost (Gregg 2019; Hernandez-Avila 2003). An example of such debate is the disagreement over indigeneity as involving biological traits, which encompass genetic characteristics that are immutable, or cultural aspects, which suggests sensibilities that be altered, suppressed, or abandoned (Gregg 2019; Tallbear 2013). Another example is the similar conceptualization of indigeneity as associated with kinship determined less by genetics and more by actions of law, ceremony, or love (Tallbear 2013).

Second, the concerns over change intersect with discussions about the nature of identity as being something static or dynamic. On one hand, an interpretation of indigeneity as a social construct incurs recognition of the interactions between actors in social networks that facilitate communication and negotiation of perceptions, ideas, and meanings related to identity. To the extent that interactions and actors within social networks are dynamic phenomena, their sensibilities regarding identity are also likely to change (Merlan 2009; Holm et al. 2003; Wilmsen & Denbow 1990). On the other hand, differentiating indigenous groups according to their respective identifiable characteristics suggests perceptions of indigeneity as involving persistent features, rendering it a static quality unlikely to change (Barnard 2006; Solway & Lee 1990). The two opposing perspectives are reflected in debates between arguments that limit indigeneity to groups exhibiting underdeveloped or traditional lifestyles, which imply an affinity to a static view of identity tied to particular modes of living, versus arguments that see indigeneity as either existing intact or becoming hybridized in developed or modern settings, which imply a belief that identity—even for a group—can retain coherence even as it changes (Barnard 2006; Guenther 2006; Kenrick 2006; Clifford 1997; Wilmsen & Denbow 1990; Solway & Lee 1990).

For both the above relational and intrinsic categories, it is also necessary to distinguish between meanings ascribed by forces external to a group or self-identified by the members of the group (Gregg 2019). Status imposed by outsiders carries colonial overtones, in that the history of colonialism involved imperial administrative structures that defined identities of subject peoples in ways that divided them into hierarchies of groups with different rights and privileges (Guenther 2006). Externally imposed identity risks essentialism, in that outsiders are describing people without necessarily understanding the nuances of their shared collective properties and are thereby subverting their freedoms to fashion a sense of self (Barnard 2006; Alfred & Corntassel 2005; Kuper 2003). Self-identification moves away from such attention to power structures and looks instead to the agency of people to craft their own sense of indigeneity (Alfred & Corntassel 2005). Self-identification is consistent with claims of self-determination, in that both involve an underlying recognition that people have capacities to declare their own priorities, create their own cultures, and compose their own identities. Moreover, they both serve an instrumental purpose of supporting group survival (Guenther 2006; Clifford 1997).

To some degree, the diversity of perspectives regarding indigeneity is not wholly divisive. It is possible for multiple conceptions of indigeneity to operate concurrently with varying degrees of overlap, coexistence, and contestation (Berger 2014). Even at the level of an individual, indigeneity can change as a function of situation in that sensibilities of identity can vary as a person transitions from one experience to another (Berger 2014). As a result, the status of indigeneity can acquire meanings crossing external–internal determinations with changing relational and intrinsic considerations specific to context. The result is a need to seek nuance that recognizes the fissures in the discourse over indigeneity and uses them to discern the differences between diverse perspectives in understanding of indigeneity.

The above complexities highlight the concept of indigeneity as a social construct between disparate viewpoints, with nuances detailing differences in interpretation (Gregg 2019; de la Cadena & Starn 2007; Alfred & Corntassel 2005). As a result, the notion of indigeneity is subjective, such that the perception of a given situation varies as a function of the diverse definitions of indigeneity used to study it (Berger 2014; Gregg 2019). To some degree, the lack of a universal definition is inevitable given the range of differences across peoples with the status of being indigenous, and in some ways, it is desirable in that it avoids the charges of essentializing nuances into an oversimplistic conceptualization incapable of illuminating the realities of lived experiences (see, for example, Barnard 2006; Kuper 2003). The absence of a universal definition, however, leaves ambiguities that challenge application of the concept of indigeneity in global discourses, particularly in international law.

Issues for international law

The ambiguities posed by the discourse over indigeneity extend to international law, which reflects the complexities in understanding as noted in the previous section. Actors and instruments in international law exhibit a range of definitions for indigeneity, with activist international NGOs, international institutions, and international instruments presenting disparate criteria despite asserting the same motivations to support the interests of indigenous peoples.

To begin, a lack of consensus is apparent among international indigenous rights NGOs, with examples of the contrast being the conceptions of Survival International and the International Work Group for Indigenous Affairs (IWGIA). Survival International, founded in 1969, describes itself as a global organization spanning more than 100 countries lobbying for the rights of those it labels as "tribes and indigenous peoples" (Survival International 2021). Its activities encompass mobilization, education, investigation, and advocacy to amplify and defend interests (Survival International 2021). Survival International defines indigenous people as those who (1) descend from populations predating the dominant or mainstream society, (2) had control of their lands taken by others, (3) are subordinate, (4) have distinctive culture, and (5) see themselves as indigenous (Survival International 2021). Tribal people are a subset of indigenous people, with additional characteristics of being dependent on land for livelihood, self-sufficient, and unassimilated into larger society (Survival International 2021). Similar to Survival International, the IWGIA has a mission of promoting and protecting indigenous rights, with focus areas on indigenous concerns with respect to land rights, global governance, territorial governance, and climate change (IWGIA 2021a). Founded in 1968, the IWGIA engages international, national, and local strategies involving advocacy, analysis, and capacity-building with partner indigenous groups in more than 90 countries (IWGIA 2021a). The IWGIA's definition of indigenous people looks to (1) habitation on land predating current states, (2) subordination in current society, (3) association of identity with location, (4) a distinctive culture, (5) self-identification as indigenous, and (6) self-determination (Coates 2004).

For its part, Survival International acknowledges the contested meaning of indigeneity, noting that "no categories of indigenous peoples are absolute" apart from the sole exception of control over land (Survival International 2021: Terminology). In contrast, while the IWGIA notes divergence across definitions regarding indigeneity, it states an aversion for essentialist theories and a preference for more pragmatic contextually specific approaches, with the main emphasis being that the concept is "formed on the basis of a discourse on rights and self-determination" (Dahl 2009: 150). In a sense, it is possible to construe some overlap between Survival International and IWGIA, in that self-determination can be interpreted as entailing self-control that includes land. Further, the two organizations also seem to share concerns regarding subordination, distinctive culture, and self-identification. Beyond those elements, however, they diverge, with Survival International including notions of descent from original inhabitants and dispossession of ancestral lands, while IWGIA instead refers to ideas of habitation predating states and attachment of identity to location.

Next, disagreement is also apparent in international institutions. Even within an entity like the United Nations (UN), where there might be an expectation of a single definition across its various branches, different interpretations have been expressed at different times by different representatives. For example, in 1982, the Special Rapporteur on the Rights of Indigenous Peoples Jose Martinez Cobo presented a separate slate of criteria involving (1) ancestry in terms of historical continuity with pre-invasion and pre-colonial societies, (2) distinction from current societies, (3) subordination, (4) desire to preserve their ancestral territories and cultures, and (5) possess their cultures, social institutions, and legal systems (Cobo 1982). Later, during his time as the head of the program for indigenous peoples and minorities at the UN Office of the High Commissioner for Human Rights (OHCHR), Julian Burger characterized the idea of indigenous people as involving criteria of (1) descent from original inhabitants overcome by conquest, (2) being nomadic or semi-nomadic, (3) lacking a central political institution, (4) being a national minority with a unique and subordinate culture, (5) holding a worldview of custodianship regarding the environment, and (6) self-identify as indigenous (Coates 2004; Burger 1987). More recently, the UN Permanent Forum on Indigenous Issues (UNPFII) affirms that there is no official UN-wide definition of indigenous peoples and goes further to argue that it is not necessary (UNPFII 2006) but also asserts that it can be understood in terms of (1) historical continuity with pre-colonial and pre-settler societies; (2) link to territory and natural resources; (3) distinctive social, economic, and political systems; (4) distinctive cultures; (5) subordinate status; (6) commitment to maintain ancestral systems; and (7) self-identification at individual and community levels (UNPFII 2021).

The above sample of institutions within the UN shares some similarities, with all three referring to ancestral continuity, subordinate status, and distinctive culture. In addition, they all mention variations of connection to land, with Burger seeing a custodian relationship, while Cobo and the UNPFII seeing it as more an association of culture with territory. However, beyond such elements they differ. The descriptions of Burger and the UNPFII include self-identification, while Cobo does not. Cobo and UNPFII both mention a resolve to preserve ancestral lands, cultures, and systems, but Burger does not. Burger looks to nomadic or semi-nomadic lifestyles, something not contained in the Cobo and UNPFII definitions. In addition, Burger sees an absence of political institutions, whereas Cobo and the UNPFII claim unique political and legal systems.

The diversity in definitions is further manifested in the international legal instruments dealing with indigenous peoples. Specifically, the International Labor Organization Convention Number 169 1989 (ILO No. 169 1989) and the United Nations Declaration on the Rights of Indigenous Peoples 2007 (UNDRIP 2007) present different approaches to the notion of indigeneity. ILO No. 169 1989 is comparable to the Survival International separation of indigenous and tribal peoples, with indigenous peoples involving (1) descent from inhabitants predating conquest, colonization, or present states; (2) retention of unique social, economic, cultural, and political institutions; and (3) self-identification as indigenous, and tribal peoples involving (1) social, cultural, and economic conditions distinct from others in their countries; (2) unique customs, traditions, or laws; and (3) self-identification as tribal (ILO 2019; ILO No. 169 1989: Art. 1). The distinction between indigenous and tribal is a choice, with the convention indicating that it is for each group of people to determine their preferred term, with the convention's text stating "Self-identification as indigenous or tribal shall be regarded as the fundamental criterion" in the application of its provisions (ILO No. 169 1989: Art. 1).

In contrast, UNDRIP adopts a different approach with no definition, stating only that "Indigenous peoples have the right to determine their own identity or membership in accordance with their customs and traditions" (UNDRIP 2007: Art. 33). The implication is a broader scope in choice relative to the ILO, with any group of people holding the full ability to generate its own conception of indigeneity. In the absence of explicit criteria, UNDRIP's language only offers guidance regarding potential characteristics that can denote indigeneity, with the preamble referencing characteristics such as concerns for colonization and dispossession of land; unique political, economic, social, cultural, and knowledge systems; discrimination and oppression; and association with territory ad resources (UNDRIP 2007: Preamble).

Both ILO No. 169 and UNDRIP assert self-determination as a central element of indigeneity, but whereas ILO No. 169 places it as preeminent among a larger list of elements, UNDRIP uses self-determination as the foundation to accord each indigenous group the power to craft its own sensibilities regarding its identity. The distinction reflects the concerns of larger discourse, particularly the arguments raised by scholarly debates over conceptions of indigeneity that are imposed upon a given group of people by forces external to the group versus those that are self-identified from the group itself. Both approaches are not without criticism. In particular, ILO No. 169 provides clarity but exposes itself to critiques that it evokes historical systems of classification that essentialized diverse communities into inflexible categories, thereby denying the agency of peoples and furthering their subjugation to hegemonic powers (Timperley 2020; Guenther 2006). In comparison, UNDRIP, in reserving definitions of identity to groups themselves, avoids essentialism in lieu of flexibility respecting the diversity and autonomy of peoples. Such flexibility, however, renders indigeneity context specific and elusive for discussions regarding transnational or transcultural indigenous issues (Timperley 2020).

Comparative conceptualizations of indigeneity

The ambiguities over indigeneity lead to a panoply of approaches. The variety of definitions is illustrated by a survey of cases across the world, which reveals the inconsistency of the concept (Canessa 2018; Levi & Maybury-Lewis 2012; Ormaza 2012; de la Cadena & Starn 2007). The following sections organize review by geographic region and states, but the selection of cases demonstrates that within each such categories, there are disparate understandings of indigeneity, and even with physically proximate cultures, there are different perspectives on the term. The demonstrated complexities highlight the nature of indigeneity as a contest over identity involving linkages between local, national, and international discourses with state and non-state actors, such that the determination of identity is specific to the scope of actors within any given context.

Forms of comparative diversity

Starting with the Americas, studies of indigenous movements in Brazil pose it as an example of multilevel political struggles going beyond the definitions set by the state (Vieira & Quack 2016). The history of peoples in the Amazon reflects several trajectories of activism allying local communities with anthropologists, Catholic clergy, and journalists against the Brazilian state, which over time crossed to produce an evolution from interpretations of indigeneity involving pre-colonial habitation or isolation toward notions of environmental stewardship and unique knowledge (Vieira & Quack 2016; French 2011; Nugent 2009; Conklin 2002). In contrast, peoples in areas now lying in Surinam and French Guiana exhibit practices that disassociate internal and external identities, with internal indigeneity prescribed by relationships that exist at locations of residence at different points in time and external indigeneity described in terms of genealogical descent (Brightman 2008). The understanding of identity can be fluid, as exemplified by Andean peoples in Ecuador and Peru whose historical pre-colonial identities were reconstructed by a Spanish colonial classification system tied to Christianity, race, and resettlement (Ogburn 2008; Stavig 2000), such that processes of "re-indigenisation" arose in relation to the formation of Amazonian–Andean alliances and connection to international environmental activism (Greene 2006). The fluidity of identity manifests in a different way in Central America, where syncretism appears in the cross-adaptation between cultures as peoples spanning El Salvador and Guatemala seek to reappropriate identities while simultaneously contending with state efforts to manipulate a Mayan narrative for tourism development and international aid efforts driving frameworks of historical continuity with distinct cultures (Rasch 2020; Tilley 2002). The reconstructions of indigenous culture involve reformulations of gender, family, community, and class (Rasch 2020). Indigeneity is also subject to migration, with indigenous groups from Mexico reconstructing their identities in the United States based on permutations of shared places of origin, ritual practices, and political claims, such that indigeneity is emblematic of self-empowerment for an instrumental purpose of engaging political institutions (Ortiz & Olavarria 2014). Continuing northward to Alaska, discourses of indigeneity place it as a function of political contestation not only against state-sponsored definitions but also between internal divisions of communities (Dombrowski 2002). Similar to such political framing are discourses in Canada, where indigeneity encompasses politics and history (Green 2009). As a result, as much as indigeneity centers around culture, treatment of land, and community continuity, it must also be recognized as emerging from the past while also being lived through the contemporary agency of various peoples against the impositions of popular culture, state domination, or forces of globalization (Green 2009). The assertion of indigeneity as contemporary politics extends to a global stage, in that indigenous agency leads to the construction of political communities outside the modern state system with attendant claims of autonomy and self-determination in the international arena (Blackburn 2009; Beier 2009; Beier 2007).

Next, proceeding across the northern space of the Arctic, the northern polar regions host peoples in lands encompassing modern states situated in the continents of North America, Europe, and Asia. The existence of the Arctic indigenous peoples is acknowledged and included within the political and legal space of the Arctic Council (Dorough 2016), but the recognition of the groups able to hold that space is contested, with different approaches to recognition arising from the diverse histories of state parties with indigenous issues within their respective borders (Sidorova 2019; Christie 2011). Within Europe, there is contestation over indigeneity with respect to the Sämi, whose historical lands cross Norway, Sweden, and Finland, with identification of who is included in the exercise of self-determination discussions involving issues of genealogical descent, cultural practice, religion, and gender (Valkonnen & Wallenius-Korkalo 2016; Beach 2007).

Similar diversity in perspectives also appears in Africa, although it appears in a context of broader claims regarding indigeneity by states covering entire populations under their jurisdiction. The justification is that under the criteria of continuity with pre-colonial populations or habitation with identifiable lands, almost everyone in Africa is indigenous (Tamuno 2017; Lutz 2007). In addition, a number of countries including Namibia, Botswana, and South Africa are reluctant to recognize special indigenous rights out of concern that it will echo the divisive historical systems of apartheid (Barnard 2019; Welch 2018; Sapignoli & Hitchcock 2013; Hays & Beisele 2011). While the underlying concern is over inequality, the focus is not necessarily on subordination of minorities since multiple states in Africa host majority populations controlled by minority elites (Bayart 1993). Despite such perspectives, there are recognized cases of claims to indigeneity. For example, in Cameroon, the nomadic Mbororo peoples identify themselves as indigenous under criteria of self-identification, distinctive culture, and marginalization and use indigeneity for instrumental purposes of addressing group interests vis-à-vis state and global levels (Pelican & Maruyama 2015). But Mbororo status is contested, in part because of a differentiation between the French colonial term *autochthone*, connoting prior arrival and bonds to specific land, versus indigenous, which is viewed as an introduction from global indigenous discourses (Pelican 2009). Cameroon state and society has given political priority to *autochthones*, particularly in regard to land rights, with the Mbororo marginalized as late-arrival pastoralists who migrated to the land from elsewhere (Pelican 2015; Pelican & Maruyama 2015). The nature of contestation is also apparent for the Khoe-San peoples, who engage in struggles for self-determination over their identity while contending with international and national discourses imposing stereotypes of "authentic" or "traditional" (Barnard 2006; Barnard 1998; Saugestad 2011; Saugestad 2001; Sylvain 2002). Within such contests, the criteria of cultural distinction and subordination become linked in that conceptions of indigenous culture are frequently framed in terms of inferiority, with the consequence that they reinforce continuing segregation and exploitation (Koot 2020; Sylvain 2002). The issue of hierarchy is not always in terms of an indigenous versus non-indigenous dichotomy. For example, the Barabaig, Hadzabe, and Maasai people of Kenya and Tanzania all self-identify as indigenous groups with unique pastoral cultures suffering common experiences of discrimination and displacement from land, but there are tensions among them arising from Barabaig and Hadzabe claims of domination by the Maasai in African and global indigenous forums and exclusion by the Maasai from access to international aid (Igoe 2006; Hodgson 2002b).

Much like the other regions above, Asia features a comparable breadth of differences in understanding of indigeneity. To some degree, Asia is closer to Africa in sharing a body of states that resist allocation of special rights for indigeneity with the reasoning that their entire populations meet the criteria for indigeneity in terms of descent from pre-colonial peoples, subordination by colonization, and continuity of cultural distinction (Baird 2016; Gerharz 2014; Hodgson 2011; Pelican 2009). In addition, claims for specific group rights are viewed as inciting intercommunal violence that permeated Asian history (Li 2002). Moreover, efforts to preserve culture or heritage are interpreted as resisting development (Kuper 2003). Further, arguments for self-determination are construed as threats to state nation-building narratives of unity, homogeneity, and nationalism (Uddin et al. 2018; Baird 2016; Clifford 2013; Erni 2008).

Despite such trends, there are disparate struggles across the region over the meaning of indigeneity. In keeping with the above trends in Asia, India eschews application of indigeneity and instead uses colonial-era notions of "tribes" or "scheduled tribes," with the Indian state applying "tribes" to groups with sociocultural identity deemed to be primitive and "scheduled tribes" to tribes listed in political-administrative categories for special treatment. Individual Indian states determine the appellation of groups and their placement in the schedule of categories (Xaxa 2016; Berger 2014). However, state ascription is contested by India's diverse population, with some groups using a Sanskrit-derived term of *adivasi* denoting themselves as being original inhabitants predating both colonization and the arrival of other cultures, and other groups adopting the English nomenclature of "indigenous people" according to their respective self-identified criteria (Xaxa 2016; Berger 2014; Karlsson 2001). With a shared colonial history, the Bangladeshi state also avoids the notion of indigeneity, preferring the term *upajatee* as an equivalent to the colonial appellation of tribes (Uddin 2019). Somewhat similar to India, a number of groups resist state ascription and choose instead to use *adivasi* in self-identifying as indigenous (Uddin 2019). Nepal, for its part, hosts discourses over the idea of indigeneity encompassing criteria of first inhabitants, unique culture, and historical territory, but similar to India, the concept is associated with "primitive" lifestyles (Paudel 2016).

The connection of indigeneity with societal hierarchy arises in different forms in Oceania and East Asia. For example, peoples in French Polynesia and New Caledonia associate the term "indigenous" with the French colonial appellation of *indigènes* that encompassed normative implications of being subhuman (Gagne 2015). While there are trends to engage the meanings of indigeneity argued by the global indigenous movement, it competes with French-language ideas of *autocthone*, with its focus on associating people with identifiable territory, and a legacy of French reluctance to recognize community rights separate from a larger community of citizens (Gagne 2015; Henriksen 2001). Concerns over hierarchy can result in the right of self-determination over identity being claimed but not exercised, with the example of the Ainu peoples in Japan demonstrating a reluctance to self-mobilize on behalf of group interests out of fear of societal discrimination, even as much as they hold a sense of solidarity and pride in being indigenous under a state recognition of their indigenous identity (Nakamura 2015). Comparable discrimination exists in the Philippines, where upland communities struggle against colonial-era stigmas that framed them as drivers of forest fires (Smith & Dressler 2020), even as the state seeks to eliminate prejudice through a suite of economic, social, political, and cultural rights for groups who self-identify themselves in terms of maintaining historical continuity with defined territory, distinctive cultures, and unique sociocultural or political-economic institutions (Theriault 2019). Contestation, however, is not always between mono-lithic dichotomies posing group self-determination against societal dis-crimination or essentialist state policies but can also arise within groups over struggles for who holds cultural or political authority to exercise collective self-determination (Paredes 2019; Theriault 2019).

In contrast to the aforementioned issues of hierarchy or group homogeneity is the aspect of fluidity. For example, the discourse of indigeneity in Taiwan involves the negotiation by peoples of identity between sensibilities toward distinctive cultural traditions, pan-Pacific geo-cultural communities predating modern state borders, resistance to Sinicization, international frameworks of indigeneity, and modernizing forces of globalization (Huang 2014; Chiu 2013). Further south, prior to colonization, the peoples of modern Indonesia existed in amorphous communities without specific group identities. Coherent group identities arose as a result of a Dutch colonial system of indirect rule which was premised on a hierarchy of tribal leaders with identifiable populations and customs (Li 2000). In post-colonial Indonesia, such group identities were subsumed into state-controlled nation-building projects that used them to target populations for development and unification programs, such that discourses of indigeneity linked cultural distinctiveness to pol-itical struggles for local visibility, resource control, and power against essentialist state programs for modernization (Tan 2020; van der Muur et al. 2019; Porath 2010; Li 2000).

The recognition of fluid identity points to ambiguities of charac-terizing groups. For example, the Bunong peoples of Cambodia and Vietnam assert a status of being indigenous but are largely silent in pre-scribing the components of Bunong indigeneity. As a result, represen-tation of what constitutes Bunong is an evolving product of activism by broader indigenous coalitions, international NGOs, diaspora communities outside Southeast Asia, and Cambodian and Vietnamese state interventions (Keating 2016). Similarly, the Akha peoples of Myanmar, Thailand, and Laos exhibit dynamic qualities arising from a migratory history tracing from Tibet and Yunnan into the upper Mekong area that incurred continually recrafted notions of their homeland, with the primary continuous thread of self-identification being a distinctive cultural cosmology (Morton et al. 2016). Within the same Mekong uplands, the Yao and Rmeet peoples also identify themselves based on cosmologies, but the Yao cosmology affirms recognition of their status by the courts of ancient imperial China, while the Rmeet cosmology emphasizes their peripheral status at the margins of Lao, Thai, Chinese, and colonial French polities (Sprenger 2013).

The coexistence of multiple understandings of indigeneity can be uneasy, with the example of Cambodia demonstrating contestation between groups who claim indigeneity as first inhabitants on the basis that they arrived on the land thousands of years in the past, groups that arrived more recently but argue for indigeneity as subordinate minorities under dominant majorities, international NGOs that define indigeneity as anyone who was colonized—not necessarily by Europeans but instead anyone, and state claims that indigeneity is lost by groups that modernize (Baird 2016). Similar contestation exists in Malaysia, where both the dominant Malay and the minority *orang asli* claim indigeneity (Gomes 2013). Both connect their identities to pre-colonial eras, but the Malay defining their status in terms of Muslim religion, a common Malay language, and distinctive Malay culture while the *orang asli* tie their status to genealogical descent from first inhabitants, distinctive culture, and marginal status (Nah 2003). The distinction is important, as under the Malaysian state's *bumiputra* system, it provides the framework of categories for the proportional distribution of rights and privileges (Cooke & Johari 2019; Nah 2003). Comparable tensions are also apparent in Thailand, where the idea of indigeneity varies between different minorities, even those within a single geographic locale (Baird et al. 2017. Complicating the discourse is the work of international activists and NGOs to promote the concept amid a contest between endemic ethno-nationalist arguments that posit state-sponsored sensibilities of "Thai-ness" against "Hill tribes" who are stigmatized as migrants driving destruction of Thai environments. In such a context, the Thai state interprets the use of indigeneity to advance group rights as being a separatist movement and so a justification to deny rights of citizenship. While the Thai state has moved toward greater recognition of distinctive cultures, it continues to deny the existence of indigenous peoples, and as a result, claims of indigeneity are predicated on asserting cultural identity compatible with a larger Thai nationalism (Morton & Baird 2019).

Trends in contestation

The preceding review of discourses regarding indigeneity demonstrates the complexities of the concept, with the meaning of indigeneity ranging across a spectrum of perspectives along an array of dimensions across the geographic scope of the world. To help clarify the complexities, it is possible to organize the above discussion along several themes demarcating fissures in understanding. First, there is a continuing legacy of colonial eras, with global discourses of indigeneity contending with disparate colonial approaches to the treatment of diverse subject peoples. The differences are apparent in the above selection of cases, which contrast the Dutch imposition of tribes upon amorphous communities; French distinctions of *indigènes*, *autochthones*, and other minorities; Spanish exercise of classes based on religion, race, and administrative settlements; and British exercise of schedules with classes of people accorded different rights. Such systems predispose post-colonial states and societies under the orientations of past colonial-era views on group identities, attendant social divisions, and consequent hierarchies. The result is that the global debates over indigeneity invariably encompass approaches applying frameworks influenced by multiple colonial legacies, with different epistemologies regarding terminology and interpretations of identity and different ontologies regarding their results.

Second, as much as a focus on distinctive culture may help to differentiate indigenous peoples from others, it is complicated by the reality of current and historical experiences. In particular, the studies of Namibia, Botswana, and South Africa noted the tendency to delineate indigenous cultures based on "authenticity" or "tradition," but both go against the fluid nature of identity and the processes by which people as individuals and groups continually reconstruct sensibilities of self and others in relation to ongoing experiences—both as acts dictated by local and global forces or as acts conducted with agency. The dynamics can lead to transformation that might be deemed modern, with the cases from Japan, Taiwan, and Indonesia illustrating how peoples can retain identities of indigeneity even as they seek to engage development programs and assume lifestyles of broader societies. In addition, the nature of change is not always toward uniqueness, with the example of syncretism across diverse cultures in El Salvador and Guatemala. The transitory nature of identity is not just longitudinal over time but also can lead to scission with coexisting multiple images, as exemplified by Surinam and French Guiana where a single group held different sensibilities of indigeneity according to situational context (Brightman 2008). The fluidity of identity reflects a constant reconstruction of self-tied to ongoing interactions between peoples interacting with surrounding forces and so challenges effort to relate indigeneity to notions of cultural continuity.

Third, following issues of cultural continuity are those of genealogical continuity. Specifically, the histories of Ecuador, Peru, and Indonesia present examples that defy the identification of genetically coherent groups. For each case, communities were amorphous, with populations and identities refashioned over time. As a result, current populations demarcating themselves as disparate indigenous communities now do not necessarily correlate to populations of the past. As a result, while it may be possible to exercise broader associations such as indigenous versus non-indigenous, more specific identification of groups can become more difficult with narrower scales of differentiation.

Fourth, attempts at basic dichotomies are vulnerable to the complexities of nuance. For example, the temporal separation between pre-colonization and colonization is contradicted by the arguments of African and Asian states who posit that their entire populations were pre-colonial. Similarly, temporal distinctions between first inhabitants versus later arrivals are frustrated by the examples of the Mbororo and Akha peoples, each of whom claim indigeneity despite being migratory cultures that arrived in lands already populated by other cultures (Morton et al. 2016; Pelican 2015; Pelican & Maruyama 2015). Dichotomies of majority versus minority or dominant versus subordinate are also problematic, with Africa hosting states with majorities controlled by minorities. Further, the examples of Kenya, Tanzania, and India point to more pluralist spaces, with domestic hierarchies spanning multiple minorities (Xaxa 2016; Berger 2014; Karlsson 2001; Igoe 2006; Hodgson 2002b). The connection of identity with hierarchies can foster intercommunal discrimination, marginalization, and exploitation and in extreme cases lead to ethnic cleansing or genocide (Nakamura 2015; Baviskar 2007; Karlsson 2003; Li 2002).

Fifth, attempts to define indigeneity with ancestral land do not operate universally. Counter-examples from the preceding discussion include the Oceania and the Pacific, where sea-based cultures populate the shorelines and archipelagos of multiple states. Even for land-based cultures, the cases of indigenous laborers traveling between Mexico and the United States, pastoralists journeying from Sahel into Cameroon, and farmers moving from China into Southeast Asia present cases where group identity persisted despite migration, with the meaning of identity evolving as people relocated to new territories. Hence, as much as it may be possible to construe indigenous peoples as having cultures with unique relationships to the natural world, ideas of connections to specific aquatic or terrestrial places are not always applicable.

Sixth, the issue of indigenous identity is not an isolated discourse, in that it occurs within a milieu of concurrent discourses addressing parallel topics. The priority and array of topics varies according to context but to the degree that they share actors interacting in common spaces they pose the potential for intersection. The preceding discussion provided multiple examples of intersectionality, such as the association of indigenous struggles with class struggle in Nepal (Paudel 2016), indigenous movements with environmental conservation in Brazil (Conklin 2002), and indigenous claims with discrimination in Japan (Nakamura 2015). Intersections can be more than dialogic, with the examples including the overlap of indigeneity, gender, and religion in Norway and Finland (Valkonnen & Wallenius-Korkalo 2016); the bridging of indigeneity, land rights, and discrimination issues with respect to pastoral communities in Kenya and Tanzania (Igoe 2006; Hodgson 2002b); and the association of indigeneity, development, and post-colonial nation-building in Indonesia and Thailand (Porath 2010; Li 2002). Richer combinations are possible, with the above review presenting complex scenarios such as Peru, with its linkages between indigeneity, race, religion, economic administration, and geography (Ogburn 2008; Greene 2006; Stavig 2000), and Taiwan, with its connections between indigeneity, pan-Pacific regionalism, relations with China, and globalization (Huang 2014; Chiu 2013). As much as intersectionality expands the scope of analysis and increases the work of investigation, it facilitates holistic understanding of the totality of context encompassing the existence of indigenous peoples. It does so by opening opportunities for cross-issue linkages, with the potential for existing actors in a discourse to take on new agenda topics or additional relationships with new actors.

Seventh, as much as struggles over indigenous identity may be specific to each individual group seeking to claim it, they can also connect to global levels in terms of reaching out to international discourses on indigeneity. Some peoples have sustained such engagements over the lifetime of the global indigenous movement, with examples like the indigenous groups from North America, Scandinavia, and Oceania delineating lead roles in advancing indigenous rights in the UN (Dahl 2012; Morgan 2007; Lindroth 2006). In other cases, such as Bolivia and Brazil, local activism worked to promote their causes as broader issues of transnational scope calling for international attention. In other cases, however, local communities followed global discourses, importing notions of indigeneity from international levels to address local struggles. Examples include Kenya, Tanzania, Namibia, South Africa, Indonesia, and Thailand, where local communities adapted international conceptions of indigeneity via direct connection to international institutions such as the UN, international NGOs, or pan-regional social movements (Baird 2016; 2019; 2020; Morton & Baird 2019; Huang 2014; Chiu 2013; Van Schendel 2002).

The above factors demarcate the fissures between diverse perspectives on indigeneity. They relate to epistemology in the sense that they identify the ways in which understanding of the term can vary, but they also pose ontological consequences in that the exercise of particular perspectives direct decisions regarding the treatment of peoples. This makes indigeneity an instrument of ulterior agendas. It is possible for agendas to manipulate indigeneity against local populations, as illustrated by the tendencies of African and Asian states to define indigeneity in ways that further systems categorizing groups in hierarchies of rights and privileges. But peoples can exercise agency to use indigeneity to advance their own interests, employing the concept to clarify their issues, frame their grievances, engage inimical forces, and access assistance from local and international actors and institutions. They do so not as proxies for foreign entities but as autonomous agents making instrumental use of indigeneity on behalf of their own agendas (Gagne 2015; Gagne 2012; Igoe 2006; Pelican 2015; Vieira & Quack 2016; Rasch 2020; Tilley 2002; Blackburn 2009; Uddin 2019; Xaxa 2016 & Karlsson 2001).

Indigeneity in Myanmar

Understanding of indigeneity as a concept in Myanmar benefits from preexisting scholarship on the country's identity politics, which presents a discourse that places discussion of indigeneity within larger contests regarding identification and status of the country's complex array of minorities. Spanning pre-colonial, colonial, and post-colonial eras, the literature largely applies terminology based on ethnicity or ethnic minorities in exploring the overlay of British administrative distinctions in the colony of Burma, maintaining the phrasing into analysis of the fractious group conflicts in the decades after independence (see, for example, Ferguson 2015, Ware & Laoutides 2018; David & Holliday 2019; Einzenberger 2016; Dittmer 2010; South 2008). In contrast, the idea of indigeneity is more relatively recent, with claims to the status of being indigenous in association with Burma appearing at least as early as 1987 in a statement delivered to the UN Working Group in Indigenous Peoples (WGIP) by Saw Mae Plet Htoo, a representative of the Karen peoples (DOCIP 2021). The scholarship on indigenous identity in Myanmar, for its part, tends to look more toward the first decades of the 21st century in investigating the shifts in identity that drove wider adoption of the term by the country's minorities in advancing rights against the Myanmar state (see, for example, Dunford 2019; Morton 2017; Thawnghmung 2016).

Saw Mae Plet Htoo's 1987 statement to the WGIP was on behalf of the Karen National Union (KNU), one of the more prominent organizations formed by the Karen peoples. In his 1987 statement, he self-identifies as indigenous and asserts the rights of the Karen as indigenous peoples to autonomy, exercising the term "indigenous nationalities" while referencing Burma's internal conflicts (DOCIP 2021). The association of indigeneity and nationality reflects the historical framing of group identities in Myanmar according to "national races" or "ethnic nationalities," a process that began under a British colonial preoccupation with categorizing the population into groups according to a hierarchy of status (Walton 2013; Myint-U 2001). In particular was the term "*taing-yin-thar*" ("တိုင်းရင်းသား"), translated as "sons of the soil" and used by the British as an indicator of eight "races" of people specific to the colonial administrative unit of Burma as distinct from anyone outside those races (Dunford 2019; Thawnghmung 2016). While applied by the British towards the distribution of rights under colonial jurisdiction, in post-independence Burma *taing-yin-thar* became subsumed in nation-building efforts that connected it with notions of origin, ethnicity, and patriotism (Waller 2020; Cheesman 2017). The consequence was a continuation of a colonial-era legacy of group division and an elevation of exclusionary tendencies, which under a military regime became associated with a goal of pacification under a dominant Bamar group majority (Morton 2017; Taylor 2015; Taylor 2009). The results are apparent in instruments such as the 1982 Citizenship Law, which employs the term *taing-yi-thar* in identifying national races or ethnic nationalities residing in Myanmar at the start of British annexation in 1823, and the 2008 Constitution, which follows the 1982 Citizenship Law in its specification of 135 national races (Myanmar Constitution 2008; ILO 2021b). The classifications are significant because they serve as a basis for determining who is eligible for citizenship, political participation, or legal protection, with unlisted groups—such as the Rohingya—subject to exclusion from Myanmar's life entirely (Morton 2017). As a result, *taing-yin-thar* is a complex term with layered meanings holding substantial implications, making its application in connection with the

English word "indigenous" a potentially problematic oversimplification (Dunford 2019).

The statement by Saw Mae Plet Htoo to the WGIP was not the only presence by Myanmar peoples in the UN and was later followed by the participation in the WGIP by a 1992 delegation from the Naga People's Movement for Human Rights (NPHMR) advocating for the Naga, a peoples spanning the border of India and Myanmar (Morton & Baird 2019), and a 1994 delegation for the Chin National Front (CNF), an ethnic armed organization (EAO) formed by Chin peoples of western Myanmar (Dunford 2019; Swift 2017). A more substantial engagement with international community, however, arose in the 2000s with the growth of Myanmar groups identifying themselves as indigenous and coalescing into national-level coalitions such as the Indigenous Peoples/ Ethnic Nationalities Network (IPEN) and the Coalition of Indigenous Peoples Myanmar (CIPM 2020). Such efforts did not occur in isolation, but instead trace back their leadership back to the 2013 efforts of the Asia Indigenous Peoples Pact (AIPP), a regional organization comprised of sub-state indigenous CSOs, to work with Myanmar ethnic groups in organizing a workshop on indigenous peoples issues for the 10th ASEAN Peoples' Forum (APF) held in 2014 in Yangon (Morton 2017). In its activities, the AIPP exhibits no organizational definition of indigeneity, with its Constitution missing a statement of criteria for the concept in describing itself as a federation of indigenous peoples organizations in Asia with membership open to all indigenous organizations in the region (AIPP 2012). Despite such ambiguity, Myanmar participants in the AIPP-affiliated workshop at the 2014 APF continued after the event to drive the development of IPEN and CIPM (Morton 2017), with both organizations advancing the status of their constituent member CSOs as indigenous peoples and advancing their claims to indigenous rights at sub-state levels within Myanmar, regional levels in broader Asia, and global levels via international institutions and sympathetic partners from other states (see, for example, CIPM 2020; IPEN 2017).

In engaging such efforts, the more recent activism by entities like IPEN and CIPM has sought to assert a conception of indigenous identity different from *taing-yin-thar*. While the appellation of *taing-yin-thar* has been casually applied as an equivalent label for the English word "indigenous" (Dunford 2019), IPEN and CIPM critique its use by arguing that (1) the meaning ascribed to *taing-yin-thar* by the 1982 Citizenship Law essentializes Myanmar diverse groups into an inaccurate whole by failing to acknowledge the subordinate status of different minorities (Morton 2017; CIPM 2015) and (2) the association of the term with national races connects to a classification system contained in the 2008 Constitution that is contested by those minorities (CIPM 2015). In its place, IPEN and CIPM have supported an alternative Burmese language term asserted *"htanay-taing-yin-thar"* ("ဌာနေ တိုင်းရင်းသား"), which they explicitly articulated in their submission to the 2021 UN Human Rights Council (HRC) UPR mechanism as

> "original dwellers who have strong ancestral ties to the present territories," based on the concept of self-identification, and using the criteria of non-dominance in the national context, historical continuity, ancestral territories, and cultural values.
>
> (CIPM 2020: 2)

The collection of such criteria evokes a pre-colonial history of minority areas that were self-governing, distinct from Burman-dominated political entities, and did not identify within any of the classifications developed by the British or later manipulated by post-independence nationalism (Dunford 2019; Steinberg 2010; Tohring 2010).

It should be noted that the above conception is not necessarily monolithic in terms of being shared in the same way by various Myanmar peoples. The literature on Myanmar's identity politics observes that some groups resist identification as indigenous peoples because of beliefs that the term connotes primitive qualities; implies a desire for special or exceptional rights rather than equality within broader society; or ties to claims of self-determination that suggest an acceptance of sub-state status and an attendant surrender of aspirations for sovereignty (Morton 2017). Even within the bounds of the preceding 2020 IPEN-CIPM submission, however, there is divergence. Specifically, an interview with a representative of Pwe-zay X (pseudonym), one of the constituent member CSOs of CIPM involved in the submission, stated a definition of indigenous peoples as "people of a country which have been long dwelling in the particular area before the country is formed" and sharing a distinct "language, culture, territory, and jurisdiction system" (Interview Pwe-zay X 2021). The interview added a belief that indigenous peoples "… have been seen as a secondary class or minority and been discriminated" (Interview Pwe-zay X 2021). Such comments evoke 2020 UPR submission's reference to non-dominance, historical continuity, ancestral territories, and identifiable culture. But the interview continued to assert that indigenous peoples have a "strong bond with its land and natural resources" and "our livelihood and socioeconomy is mainly based on land and forest" (Interview Pwe-zay X 2021), indicating another criterion of a special relationship with the natural world. The consequence is that as much as the IPEN-CIPM

2020 submission may have sought to represent a consistent definition of indigeneity shared across their constituent member CSOs, at least one of those CSOs held a different understanding. The subsequent implication is one of agency, with an individual CSO like Pwe-zay X participating within a broader coalition presenting a conception of indigeneity in the 2020 UPR submission even as it concurrently held its own interpretation of the term.

For its part, the Myanmar state has demonstrated a reluctance to follow recognition of indigeneity expressed in international discourses. In particular, it is not a state party to ILO No. 169 (ILO 2021a), and while it voted in support of UNDRIP, it holds to position that all peoples in Myanmar are indigenous and hence there is no need to implement special rights for minorities (Morton 2017). There has been some movement toward positions consistent with indigenous rights without express recognition of idea of indigenous rights, with the examples of the 2015 Ethnic Rights Protection Law (ERPL) going so far as to use "*htanay-taing-yin-thar*" in providing rights on culture, development, political participation, and free prior informed consent comparable to components of ILO No. 169 and UNDRIP, and the 2016 National Land Use Policy (NLUP) calling for greater protection of customary land tenure (Morton 2017). For the ERPL, however, the Myanmar state asserts an interpretation of "*htanay-taing-yin-thar*" as meaning "local ethnic nationalities" and the NLUP similarly ties customary forms of land use to ethnic nationalities (Morton 2017). Moreover, more recent legislation such as the 2018 Forest Law and 2018 Conservation of Biodiversity and Protected Areas Law omit the term "*htanay-taing-yin-thar*" entirely (Liljeblad et al. 2021).

Implications

The preceding analysis of indigeneity in Myanmar poses implications for the position of its meaning not just within the country but also relative to larger international discourses. The delineation of the concept's growth in Myanmar also presents additional implications regarding the relationship between Myanmar indigenous rights movements and international actors like the AIPP. Each set of implications is addressed in separate subsections below.

International and comparative conceptions

As much as the definition claimed by groups like IPEN and CIPM for *htanay-taing-yin-thar* deal with the experiences of their constituent members, they also connect to the conceptions of indigeneity in international discourses. The reference was explicit in their 2015 submission to the UN HRC UPR, which stated that they use *htanay-taing-yin-thar* "based on the international concept" and call "for a national-level dialogue to identify and recognize indigenous peoples in Myanmar/Burma, based on the international concept and the UNDRIP" (CIPM 2015: 3). However, as summarized by the discussion of previous sections, the term "international" may indicate perspectives present in global-level spaces or in comparison between country contexts. The notions of Myanmar indigeneity are placed in relation to each below.

With respect to global discourses, as much as the 2015 UPR submission states UNDRIP alongside mention of an international concept, it is possible to identify the connections between the IPEN and CIPM definition of *htanay-taing-yin-thar* with a range of international definitions of indigeneity exercised by the NGOs, international organizations, and international law summarized in earlier in the present chapter. To begin, the criterion of historical continuity fits as one of the elements characterizing indigeneity held by Survival International (2021) and similarly the criterion of ancestral lands matches one of the elements noted by IWGIA (2021a). The criteria of self-identification, marginal status, and unique culture align with components shared in the definitions of indigeneity held by the two organizations (IWGIA 2021a; Survival International 2021). In terms of definitions held by international institutions, the five criteria prescribed by IPEN and CIPM fall short of the elements raised by Julian Burger for the OHCHR in that they do not address his expectations for nomadic or semi-nomadic lifestyles nor custodianship of the environment (Coates 2004; Burger 1987). But they do fall readily within the requirements offered by Jose Martinez Cobo as Special Rapporteur on the Rights of Indigenous Peoples (Cobo 1982) and the example guidelines offered by the UNPFII (2021), which include all five of the criteria within their respective descriptions of indigeneity.

With respect to definitions in international law, the components of self-identification, historical continuity, and unique culture are contained with the ILO No. 169 characteristics for indigenous or tribal peoples. Further, and in keeping with the reference to UNDRIP in the 2015 IPEN and CIPM submission to the UPR, the exercise of self-determination underlying the IPEN and CIPM prescription for the criteria of *htanay-taing-yin-thar* fits wholly within the UNDRIP's assertion of indigenous peoples holding "the right to determine their own identity or membership" (UNDRIP 2007: Art. 33). As a result, the assertion of *htanay-taing-yin thar* bridges the identity politics discourses of Myanmar indigenous activists with the global discourses of indigeneity, opening avenues to address domestic grievances through international mechanisms open to indigenous rights claims.

In regard to cross-country contexts, comparison of the IPEN and CIPM notion of *htanay-taing-yin-thar* with the comparative trends identified previously in the chapter indicates some contrasts in perceptions regarding indigeneity. First, the history of Myanmar minorities is consistent with the theme of colonial legacy, in that the marginal status of Myanmar peoples claiming indigeneity is affected by British colonial era practices of classification and hierarchical distribution of rights that were co-opted in post-independence to further interests of nation-building under military rule. Second, the definition of *htanay-taing-yin-thar* in the 2021 UPR submission includes a claim of historical continuity, which suggests an ongoing self-identification as a distinct group. The mention of cultural values indicates that such self-identification of shared history involves cultural continuity. But associating historical continuity with cultural continuity contrasts with the cases demonstrating fluidity and syncretism, placing Myanmar more in alignment with contexts where indigeneity was viewed as denoting cultures identifiable by their authenticity or tradition. Third, apart from history and culture, the definition *htanay-taing-yin-thar* makes no reference to genealogical continuity, positioning indigenous peoples in Myanmar among indigenous histories with amorphous genetics. Fourth, to some degree, Myanmar indigenous discourse conforms to patterns of dichotomy, with distinctions including indigenous versus non-indigenous and Bamar majority versus non-Bamar minority, but the constituent members of both IPEN and CIPM also suggest claims to indigeneity by multiple peoples and so present a pluralist space of differing identities. Fifth, the definition in the 2021 UPR submission makes a clear mention of ancestral territories and so fits directly with cases where indigenous peoples claim belonging to identifiable areas of land. Sixth, Myanmar's discourse over indigeneity mirrors those cases exhibiting cross-issue contestation, with the claims of indigenous rights in Myanmar intersecting with historical struggles for autonomous self-governance and group identity independent of colonial or post-independence systems of classification and driving current issues of human rights and environment. Last, the relationship between the Myanmar indigenous activists with entities like the AIPP and IWGIA conforms to the experiences of other contexts where local peoples worked with international actors in mobilizing indigenous movements, importing ideas of indigeneity and attendant indigenous rights from existing discourses in international institutions and other countries.

Intermediaries

The lineages of IPEN and CIPM trace their respective leadership to AIPP-organized workshop on indigenous rights at the 2014 APF. The activities of the AIPP in working with representatives of Myanmar ethnic groups in preparation for the workshop, and the subsequent contributions of those representatives in the formation of IPEN and CIPM following the workshop, point to a role played by the AIPP in promoting awareness of ideas regarding indigeneity. While AIPP itself does not prescribe a particular understanding of indigeneity, its efforts gave some measure of impetus that led to IPEN and CIPM formulating a preferred translation of *htanay-taing-yin-thar* with a specific definition involving a list of criteria evocative of definitions for indigeneity held in international discourses. Such influence follows the notions of intermediaries as facilitating the spread of information between local and global levels (Bettiza & Dionigi 2015; Golan & Or 2012; Merry 2006), with AIPP serving to connect local activists in Myanmar to larger international discussions regarding indigenous peoples and conveying information that contributed to the growth of Myanmar indigenous rights movements.

In the case of Myanmar indigenous activists, however, agency was not solely with the AIPP as intermediary. In particular, the preceding section indicates agency by Myanmar groups in two ways. First, the statement of a specific definition for indigeneity in their 2020 UPR submission indicates an ability by IPEN and CIPM to construct their own meaning for the idea in the absence of a definition from AIPP. Second, the deviation from the 2020 UPR submission definition given by Pwezay X points to additional ability of constituent member CSOs within IPEN and CIPM to form their own interpretations of indigeneity apart from other Myanmar partners. The parallels between such local understandings with descriptions in international discourses, particularly in reference to such sources as UNDRIP, suggest that Myanmar indigenous activists are also capable of using and refashioning international perspectives into their own unique phrasings of indigeneity. Hence, as much as Myanmar peoples may have been the recipient of ideas and meanings from an amorphous international discourse on indigeneity, they are able to exercise agency in selecting sources within that discourse to form their own approaches to indigenous identity.

Conclusion

The preceding sections explored the nature of indigeneity in Myanmar, identifying the conceptions of Myanmar indigenous CSOs and locating their place within larger global discussions on the notion of indigeneity. While Myanmar indigenous activists have expressed their own identifiable definitions for indigeneity, they do so in reference to concepts chosen from a larger international discourse. Such efforts, however, are not entirely for purposes of identity, with the subsequent chapters addressing how Myanmar indigenous CSOs connected their status as indigenous peoples to claims of rights in the UPR and UNFCCC. To the extent that indigeneity was a vehicle for complaints to both mechanisms, it served an instrumental purpose of accessing human rights and environmental rights available in institutions of international law. The next chapters investigate the manner of Myanmar indigenous engagement with the UPR and UNFCCC, extending the work of the above sections to ascertain the ways in which Myanmar indigenous CSOs used the UPR and UNFCCC to address their local concerns with the Myanmar state. Building upon the present analysis, the next chapters draw further implications for understanding the agency of indigenous peoples in engaging international institutions and rules.

3 Myanmar Indigenous Engagement with the United Nations Human Rights Council Universal Periodic Review

The Coalition of Indigenous Peoples in Myanmar (CIPM) made its first engagement with Universal Periodic Review (UPR) mechanism during its 2015 session to evaluate Myanmar (Snaing 2015). A process hosted by the United Nations (UN) Human Rights Council (HRC), the UPR exercises a cycle that reviews the human rights record of each UN member state approximately every five years (OHCHR 2021a; UNGA 2007b; UNGA 2006). Following such a pattern, the CIPM repeated its involvement for the UPR session on Myanmar in 2021 (OHCHR 2021b; OHCHR 2021c). For both sessions, the CIPM submitted reports which asserted indigenous concerns regarding the environment (HRC 2021c; CIPM 2020; HRC 2015; CIPM 2015), marking attempts to use an international human rights mechanism to address sub-state domestic indigenous issues. Such an approach is consistent with a larger trends to recognize connections between environmental and human rights topics (Boer 2015; Grear & Kotze 2015). Since its inception, the UPR has become an inclusive process open to hearing human rights issues arising from a range of subjects, including environmental problems (Bureau des Avocats Internationaux 2011; Grear & Kotze 2015) and indigenous complaints (Anaya 2012; Cultural Survival 2015; IWGIA 2015). In particular, the use of the UPR to address environmental issues is recognized as an acceptable exercise by the United Nations Office of the High Commissioner for Human Rights (OHCHR) (HRC 2013). With respect to Myanmar, there have been multiple submissions to the UPR from different actors that have framed environmental issues as human rights violations (ICJ 2015; IHRB 2015). The CIPM's submissions constitute a formal attempt by indigenous peoples in Myanmar to engage an international human rights mechanism to address local indigenous grievances regarding the environment.

By reaching out to an international mechanism to address local problems, the CIPM is following an approach advocated by indigenous

DOI: 10.4324/9781003133728-3

rights organizations such as the International Work Group on Indigenous Affairs (IWGIA). The IWGIA has noted a growing trend of indigenous participation in the UPR and encourages indigenous peoples to use the UPR as a tool to advance their interests (IWGIA 2015; IWGIA 2011). This activity is consistent with larger patterns of non-state actors pursuing transnational actions (Brysk 2000; Keck & Sikkink 1998; Risse et al. 1999) and expanding their roles across domestic and global levels of governance (Guidry et al. 2000; Held & McGrew 2002; Scholte 2002).

This chapter evaluates the CIPM engagement with the UPR. This chapter argues that CIPM approaches to the UPR reflect sophistication in terms of linking multiple issues and multiple strategies in a systematic campaign which fashioned indigenous concerns for local environmental problems as human rights issues under the purview of an international human rights mechanism. Such complexities go beyond the apparent simplicity of CIPM's use of the UPR and reflect a broader range of elements inherent in indigenous efforts to engage in global discourses. The discussion begins with a summary of the theory of transnational advocacy networks (TANs) that describes the nature of CIPM's outreach to the UPR process, along with a brief statement regarding the methodology. The discussion then provides a background regarding the CIPM, indigenous peoples in Myanmar, and the UPR. The analysis proceeds to discuss the findings of fieldwork, drawing upon statements of a participating member of the CIPM to identify issues in its engagement with the UPR. The analysis follows by identifying the significance of the findings for theories of transnational indigenous activism.

Theory and methodology

The exercise of the UPR mechanism by CIPM conforms to the "Boomerang Pattern" model introduced by Margaret Keck and Kathryn Sikkink (1998). Generally, the Boomerang Pattern describes situations where a state is unresponsive to the concerns of domestic actors and those actors appeal to the international community to pressure the unresponsive state into addressing the domestic concerns (Keck & Sikkink 1998). The term "domestic" indicates sub-state actors under the jurisdiction of a state, and "international" refers to actors outside such jurisdiction encompassing non-state actors, international institutions, and other states (Keck & Sikkink 1998). The Boomerang Pattern falls within the wider scholarship on TANs, which are defined by Keck and Sikkink as "networks of activists, distinguishable largely by the centrality of principled ideas or values in motivating their formation" (Keck & Sikkink 1998: 1). The identifying characteristics of a TAN are "actors working internationally on an issue, who are bound together by shared values, a common discourse, and dense exchanges of information and services" (Keck & Sikkink 1998: 2). The power of a TAN arises from the capacities of its members to "mobilize information strategically to create new issues and categories and to persuade, pressure, and gain leverage over much more powerful organizations and governments" (Keck & Sikkink 1998: 2).

The notion of TANs was originally posed in relation to issues of indigenous rights, human rights, and environment (Keck & Sikkink 1998) but has spawned a wide-ranging literature denoting varying forms of the Boomerang Pattern in areas of labor (Trubek et al. 2000), children's rights (Carpenter 2007), climate change (Ciplet 2014), corporate conduct (McAteer & Pulver 2009), education (Mundy & Murphy 2001), environmental protection (Huelshoff & Christina 2012; Wiedener 2009), human rights (Risse et al. 1999), indigenous rights (Rodrigues 2004; Wright 2014); independence movements (Noakes 2012), public health (Wu 2005), sexual harassment (Zippel 2004), and women's rights (Sperling et al. 2001). The literature has found the Boomerang Pattern extending beyond issue-specific confines, with networks capable of hosting activists engaged in cross-issue linkages. In particular, scholars like Kathryn Hochstetler, Margaret Keck, and Pamela Martin have posed cases where indigenous activists addressed domestic environmental struggles against a state by reaching out to international actors (Hochstetler & Keck 2007; Martin 2011; Martin 2003). As a result, TANs and the Boomerang Pattern offer a means of understanding the work of Myanmar's indigenous peoples to use an international mechanism like the UPR to address their concerns with the Myanmar state.

Application of the Boomerang Pattern model to the present study requires several notes regarding methodology. First, the focus of the study on CIPM's use of UPR constitutes a case study, with the bounds of the case set by the CIPM as an organization and the 2015 and 2021 UPR sessions on Myanmar as the iterations of the UPR involving the CIPM (CIPM 2020; CIPM 2015). Second, the analysis draws on primary and secondary source documents, field notes, and interviews collected during the period of fieldwork 2015–2020. Third, with respect to field notes and interviews, the following sections are mindful of the comments in Chapter 1 regarding the need to protect the identities of sources on indigenous, human rights, and environmental issues in Myanmar. To a degree, the risks of inferring identities are mitigated by the membership numbers for the CIPM, which encompasses a current total of 28 civil society organizations (CSOs) that provide a number of potential sources sufficient to challenge any attempts to associate data with specific sources. The analysis, however, also works to reduce the risks of potential identification by anonymizing data, using pseudonyms, and removing information that might indicate sources. Moreover, the analysis seeks to further reduce the risks of identification by minimizing the use of field notes and interviews whenever possible in lieu of data already available in publicly accessible documents within scholarly databases, news media, UN records, and reports of CSOs and non-governmental organizations (NGOs). Last, the following sections also observe the notes in Chapter 1 regarding the fluid conditions in Myanmar during the period of fieldwork, and the analysis mitigates their complexities by confining the scope of study to the CIPM's experience with the UPR, such that larger issues enveloping indigenous peoples in Myanmar are filtered in terms of their association with the CIPM as it sought to use the UPR in relation to the environmental grievances of CIPM's indigenous constituencies.

Background

In studying the CIPM engagement with the UPR as a form of TANs, it is helpful to contextualize the analysis in terms of background regarding the CIPM and Myanmar. With respect to the CIPM, the organization began in 2015 with an initial membership of 24 indigenous CSOs with the express purpose of representing their collective interests at the UPR Working Group sessions reviewing Myanmar (OHCHR 2021c; CIPM 2020; HRC 2015). As an umbrella entity for its CSO constituents, the CIPM works on a consultative basis that organizes members into thematic working groups, each of which produces content that is then circulated to the larger membership for consultation. Using consultation feedback, the collective applies majority consensus to generate submission reports for the UPR Working Group sessions (CIPM 2020). The CIPM's first submission was to the 23rd Session of the UPR Working Group during its review of Myanmar in 2015 (CIPM 2015; HRC 2015). It made a second submission to the 37th Session of the UPR Working Group during its review of Myanmar in 2021 (OHCHR 2021c; HRC 2021c; CIPM 2020).

The outreach by the CIPM to the UPR was motivated by the frustrations of its member CSOs with the Myanmar state in dealing with their collective concerns. In particular, in the submissions to the above UPR Working Group sessions, the members of the CIPM asserted the failure of the Myanmar state in addressing the suppression of their claims to self-determination, loss of their traditional lands, injuries to historical natural resources, and accompanying violations of human rights (HRC 2021c; CIPM 2020; CIPM 2015; HRC 2015). In turning to the UPR, the members of the CIPM sought international assistance to encourage the Myanmar state to become more responsive to the ongoing struggles with the aforementioned issues.

The complaints of CIPM members reflect a number of endemic problems with the Myanmar state. To begin, the Myanmar state is reluctant to adopt the concepts of "indigenous peoples" or "indigenous rights." The concept of "indigenous" is a relatively recent introduction in Myanmar, with ongoing efforts involving various foreign NGOs and local CSOs to promote understanding of the term (Liljeblad 2018; POINT 2015). While the Myanmar state acknowledged the general ideas of indigenous peoples and indigenous rights by voting in favor of the UN Declaration on the Rights of Indigenous Peoples (UNDRIP) (UNGA 2007a), it does not formally apply either one in Myanmar laws, maintaining instead the notion of "national races" contained in the 2008 Constitution (Myanmar Constitution 2008) or the term "*taing-yin-thar*" ("တိုင်းရင်းသား," indicating ethnic groups present at the start of British annexation in 1823) in the 1982 Citizenship Law (ILO 2021b; CIPM 2015). Both terms differ from the words preferred by CIPM, which uses the phrase "*htanay-taing-yin-thar*" ("ဌာနေတိုင်းရင်းသား") to denote people who self-identify as a group holding marginal status, historically continuous identity, identifiable ancestral territory, and claims to self-determination (CIPM 2015).

The Myanmar state's aversion to the ideas of indigenous peoples or indigenous rights relates to the country's chronically fractured political environment, which hosts an array of ethnic and indigenous groups with diverse claims of sovereignty driving a civil war that has continued since the country's independence in 1948 (Oo 2015; Mitchell 2013). While civilian governments during 2010–2021 held peace talks, the country continues to struggle with a pluralist terrain of political interests contesting what Larry Diamond described as issues regarding the path "from authoritarianism to democracy, from military to civilian rule, from a closed and monopolistic to an open and competitive economy, and from an ethnically fractured and fissiparous state to a more viable and coherent union" (Callahan 2012; Diamond 2012; Egreteau 2014; Joseph 2012). The diverse factions are not entirely peaceful, with the country still hosting multiple conflicts with a myriad of ethnic armed organizations (EAOs) fighting to advance their respective interests for varying degrees of autonomy (Jolliffe 2015; Kramer 2015; Farrelly 2014). The persistence of conflict fosters instability, with continuing tensions between a Myanmar state striving to increase unity through centralized control and indigenous communities seeking to fulfill historical claims of self-determination (Kramer 2015; Farrelly 2014; Taylor 2009).

Beyond the desultory progress on indigeneity or peace-building, the Myanmar state also suffers from problems of underdevelopment driving lack of capacity and weak rule of law. With respect to underdevelopment, the World Bank listed Myanmar's annual Gross National Income per capita in 2020 at US$4,650, ranking it 142 out of 188 measured countries (World Bank 2021). The UN Human Development Report for 2020 gives Myanmar a Human Development Index score of 0.583, placing it 147th out of 188 countries (UNDP 2020). Myanmar's poverty has left a state bereft of capacity across all areas at all levels, with weak institutions, opaque leadership, dysfunctional civil service, poor infrastructure, inadequate resources, and insufficient skills (Chalk 2013; Cheesman et al 2012; Crouch & Lindsey 2014; Nixon et al. 2013). Attendant with weak capacity are problems with corruption and poor rule of law. In 2020, Transparency International's Corruption Perceptions Index listed Myanmar 137th out of 175 countries (Transparency International 2020). Similarly, the World Justice Project, in calculating its Rule of Law Index assessing constraints on government powers, absence of corruption, security, observance of rights, and enforcement, ranked Myanmar 112th out of 128 countries (World Justice Project 2020). The convergence of poverty, lack of capacity, corruption, and weak rule of law render Myanmar a space with limited means to support any potential will the state may have to address the interests of indigenous peoples.

Overshadowing all of the above concerns is the presence of Myanmar's military, or Tatmadaw, which has driven the country into authoritarianism and isolationism responsible for much of its current problems (Nakanishi 2013; Taylor 2009; Callahan 2003). Even during the period of civilian governments from 2010 to 2021, the military maintained a lurking threat against the country's efforts at democratic reforms and economic liberalization. As indicated in a January 2015 interview with Channel News Asia, military leader General Min Aung Hlaing stated that the military was reluctant to reduce its role in government, claiming that it was necessary to maintain stability (Channel News Asia 2015a; Channel News Asia 2015b; Channel News Asia 2015c). More ominously, he placed stability as a higher priority than political or economic reform and refused to rule out the resumption of military control over the country (Channel News Asia 2015a; Channel News Asia 2015b; Channel News Asia 2015c). Such sentiments were realized in February 2021, when the Tatmadaw conducted a military coup that removed the elected civilian government, declared a state of emergency, and launched a campaign to eliminate political resistance (Liljeblad 2022; *The Guardian* 2021a; *The Guardian* 2021d). The restoration of military rule incurred a popular uprising, with widespread street protests, civil disobedience across all ministries at all levels of government, and resumption of conflict by EAOs (Liljeblad 2022; *The Guardian* 2021b; *The Guardian* 2021c). The response of the Tatmadaw has been a declaration of martial law with increased restrictions on protest, reduced access to internet, arrests and detentions, and torture and killings of unarmed civilians (Bloomberg 2021; *The Guardian* 2021a).

Myanmar's endemic problems impede its performance with respect to international human rights norms, with the military's conduct in the wake of the February 2021 coup only extending the country's historical deficit on human rights. Under the civilian governments from 2010 to 2021, Myanmar made a modicum of progress, with the formation of the Myanmar National Human Rights Commission and ratification of the Convention on the Rights of Persons with Disabilities, two Protocols to the Convention on the Rights of the Child, and the International Covenant on Economic, Social, and Cultural Rights (UN 2021d; APF 2015). Despite such efforts, however, the UN continued to observe ongoing human rights issues, with the UN regularly renewing the mandate of Special Rapporteur on the Status of Human Rights in Myanmar (OHCHR 2021d). The reports of the Special Rapporteur since its inception in 1992 present a record of chronic inability to meet international human rights norms across a swath of issues, with widespread violations crossing topics of minority rights, gender rights, religious rights, land rights, free speech, free press, free assembly, equality, rights against arbitrary arrest and detention, right against torture, right to life, right to health, right to education, and right to culture (OHCHR 2021d; UNGA 2021; UNGA 2020; UNGA 2015a; UNGA 2015b; UNGA 2015c; UNGA 2014). As much as events since the February 2021 coup escalated human rights concerns and drew heightened condemnation from the international community (OHCHR 2021e; UNSC 2021; *Washington Post* 2021), Myanmar's past indicates a state with perpetually anemic performance on human rights. As a result, to the extent that the CIPM tried to frame Myanmar indigenous grievances within the concepts of human rights for the 2015 and 2021 UPR Working Group sessions on Myanmar, during that time period Myanmar's indigenous peoples were facing conditions generally inhospitable to their concerns.

Referencing the notion of TANs set by Keck and Sikkink, the use of the UPR by the CIPM is consistent with their Boomerang Pattern model. Specifically, a number of indigenous CSOs in Myanmar were

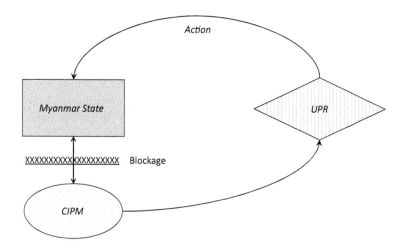

Figure 3.1 The "Boomerang Pattern" for CIPM (Adapted from
    Liljeblad 2018).

frustrated by a perceived anemic response from the Myanmar government regarding the degradation of their environment, with indigenous groups arguing that the government was responsible, complicit,
or incapacitated with respect to projects harming their land and natural resources. Faced with an unresponsive state, these CSOs allied
together as the CIPM to engage the HRC's UPR mechanism, effectively
reaching out to an international institution and its processes to pressure
greater action by the Myanmar state. Hence, to the extent that the UPR
involves UN member states, UN agencies or NGOs from other countries, the CIPM's use of the UPR involved accessing a transnational network of relationships exchanging information and performing services
with respect to the conduct of the Myanmar government in relation to
UN standards of human rights. Thus, following Keck and Sikkink, the
CIPM formed a Boomerang Pattern of transnational advocacy on its
behalf. An illustration of the Boomerang Pattern in the case of CIPM's
use of the UPR is given by Figure 3.1.

Findings

The CIPM's experiences with the UPR mechanism center around its
activities in the preparation and submission of reports identifying
Myanmar indigenous complaints against the conduct of the Myanmar

state. There were two reports, with the first CIPM report for the UPR Second Cycle review of Myanmar held during the Working Group's 23rd session in 2015 and the second CIPM report for the UPR Third Cycle review of Myanmar conducted by the Working Group's 37th session in 2021 (CIPM 2020; CIPM 2015). Both reports, along with the summaries of the deliberations for both sessions published by the Working Group (HRC 2021c; HRC 2015), provide a record indicating how the CIPM framed Myanmar indigenous concerns as human rights issues under the purview of the UPR mechanism.

For the 23rd session in 2015, the CIPM's claims covered a range of issues encompassing themes of land, natural resources, development, self-determination, and human rights (CIPM 2015; HRC 2015). The central driver of such issues was the environmental damage resulting from dam building, road construction, plantation clearing, mining, and timber, all of which frequently involved the confiscation or exploitation of indigenous land in ways that violated international and domestic expectations for effective remedies; environmental impact assessments; and free, prior, informed consent (FPIC) (CIPM 2015; HRC 2015). Beyond the aforementioned procedural issues, the CIPM highlighted the substantive consequences of the above projects in the form of violations of indigenous collective rights to subsistence, cultural practices, and customary laws related to their land (CIPM 2015; HRC 2015). In addition, because decisions about the land occurred without negotiation or notification from the government, they also violated indigenous rights to self-determination (CIPM 2015; HRC 2015). Further, many of these projects involved the replacement of indigenous names in lieu of Burmese language terms and the destruction of sites of cultural significance to indigenous peoples and so violated indigenous rights regarding cultural heritage (CIPM 2015). Moreover, because the government worked to suppress indigenous efforts to organize public protests or access legal protections against such projects, it violated rights of free speech, free assembly, equality under the law, and access to the law (CIPM 2015; HRC 2015). Last, because many of the extractive industries and large-scale agriculture produce toxic waste, they threatened the right to life (CIPM 2015; HRC 2015). Exacerbating the slate of issues raised by the CIPM was the lack of recognition for indigenous rights by the Myanmar state, which claimed that all people in Myanmar were indigenous and hence undeserving of special rights protections (HRC 2015).

CIPM's grievances continued with similar themes for the 37th session in 2021, with the CIPM's submission to the UPR asserting that despite the introduction of new Myanmar laws, there continued to be problems regarding land, natural resources, self-determination, and human rights (HRC 2021c; CIPM 2020). The drivers were expanded to include mega-projects and conflict, both of which incurred dispossession or destruction of indigenous lands and natural resources (CIPM 2020). In addition, land-grabbing was complemented by complaints of "green-grabbing" wherein the Myanmar state cited its obligations to international environmental treaties as justifications to seize indigenous lands (CIPM 2020). Within its submission, the CIPM raised procedural issues regarding violations of rights to FPIC, rights against arbitrary detentions and enforced disappearances, rights on access to justice, and rights for effective redress (HRC 2021c; CIPM 2020). In addition, it also claimed substantive issues in terms of violations of rights to equality, subsistence, culture and cultural heritage, health services, and education (HRC 2021c; CIPM 2020). However, it went further beyond its 2015 UPR submission to identify the dangers to indigenous and environmental human rights defenders, signaling an explicit connection between indigenous rights, human rights, and environment (HRC 2021c; CIPM 2020). Finally, the CIPM's submission noted that while the Myanmar government had started to informally reference ideas of indigenous identity and indigenous rights, it failed to recognize either one in domestic laws (HRC 2021c; CIPM 2020). The CIPM asserted that Myanmar's new laws continued to fall short of international norms and failed to address the concerns of CIPM's constituencies (HRC 2021c; CIPM 2020).

The content of the CIPM's submissions to the 2015 and 2021 UPR Working Group sessions on Myanmar demonstrate a linking of human rights and environmental arguments to address indigenous issues. In both submissions, the CIPM raised indigenous concerns with respect to land and natural resources, placing such concerns in relation to human rights violations by the Myanmar state. The nature of human rights problems was multidimensional in the sense of encompassing both procedural and substantive aspects as well as contrasting domestic Myanmar laws with international norms. The motivations of CIPM's submissions were more than descriptive, with each report prescribing recommendations to rectify their respective grievances. While the recommendations were directed to the Myanmar state, their call for action by the UN Special Rapporteur on the Rights of Indigenous Peoples (CIPM 2015) and UN Permanent Forum on Indigenous Issues (CIPM 2020); reference to the UN Declaration of Rights of Indigenous Peoples 2007 (CIPM 2020; CIPM 2015); and submission to the UPR mechanism indicate an effort by the CIPM to appeal to the UN system for assistance. As such, they illustrates a CIPM strategy of cross-issue linkages, with its constituent members addressing local concerns regarding natural resources through an exercise of indigeneity and corresponding claims to indigenous lands associated with various human rights recognized by international law. Such linkages enabled the CIPM to present the grievances of its members as a submission to the international human rights mechanism of the UPR.

Despite the depth of CIPM's efforts in preparing its reports for the UPR Working Group sessions, the strategy vis-à-vis the UPR encountered issues that frustrated their submission. Specifically, the CIPM's experiences with the UPR mechanism indicate that it was not a straightforward process, with field data revealing issues that affected the working of the Boomerang Pattern. For purposes of clarity, it is helpful to organize the data according to issues of engagement, access, and outcomes. Issues of engagement refer to the complexities that confronted CIPM during their involvement with the UPR process. Issues of access relate to problems that challenged CIPM's preparations to initiate the use of the UPR. Issues of outcomes encompass the consequences for CIPM interests that resulted from UPR deliberations. Each is summarized in the respective subsections below.

Issues of engagement

The CIPM encountered issues in engagement in the form of restrictions upon its participation as a non-state actor in UPR proceedings. The CIPM's efforts involved the submission of reports regarding Myanmar state conduct toward indigenous peoples to the 2015 and 2021 UPR Working Group sessions on Myanmar. As part of the report submissions, the CIPM sent representatives to the UPR Working Group site in Geneva. The justification for doing so was summarized by Pwe-zay Y (pseudonym), who was one of the representatives who traveled to the 2015 Working Group session: "Apart from writing and submitting the report, it is important our issues are addressed or questioned by the delegates in the UPR reviewing session" (Interview Pwe-zay Y 2021). When they were physically on-site in Geneva, the CIPM summarized each report as one-page paper facts sheet and distributed it to diplomats. They also "arranged and conducted side event inviting delegates" interested in Myanmar issues (Interview Pwe-zay Y 2021). An underlying theme across such comments is that the nature of engagement in the UPR did not mean real-time physical participation in the discussions of Working Group sessions but rather involved separation in the form of written submissions or events outside the Working Group proceedings. In which case, for the CIPM engagement constituted of limited communications indirectly conveyed to Working Group deliberations.

The limitations of engagement by the CIPM reflect the design of the UPR process. In brief, the UPR process exercises a sequence of four steps: (1) the submission of information in the form of reports about a state's human rights record from UN bodies, UN member states, national human rights institutions (NHRIs), and NGOs; (2) a Working Group meeting involving discussions based on the submitted reports to evaluate the given state's progress toward the standards of the UN human rights system; (3) the publication of an outcome report at the end of the Working Group meeting containing recommendations to improve the reviewed state's status on human rights; and (4) subsequent provision of capacity-building and technical aid, along with the exercise monitoring measures, directed at helping the reviewed state fulfill the outcome report recommendations (OHCHR 2021a). The Working Group meetings involve the 47 member states of the HRC, led by a troika selected by drawing lots from the HRC members (OHCHR 2021a). In reviewing the human rights performance of a particular state, the Working Group exercises an interactive format involving questions, answers, and comments between the Working Group members and the state under review (OHCHR 2021a). At the end of each Working Group session, the Working Group troika leadership works with the OHCHR and the reviewed state to generate an "outcome report" that presents the queries, observations, and recommendations made by all participants present during the Working Group proceedings. The report also includes the responses of the reviewed state, including its decision to either accept or note the recommendation (OHCHR 2021a). The outcome report is then given to the HRC plenary for deliberation, where all UN member states, their affiliated NHRIs, and NGOs are allowed to make additional questions and comments, and the reviewed state is once again allowed to reply. Once the HRC finalizes and adopts the report, the responsibility for action shifts to the reviewed state to implement the accepted recommendations of the report in time for the next review, at which time it is expected to explain to what extent and why it has satisfied or failed to fill the recommendations (OHCHR 2021a).

There is a disparity in the privileges accorded to states and non-state actors in the Working Group sessions. Any state that is a member of the UNGA is allowed to submit reports for Working Group consideration, pose questions and comments in the Working Group discussions, and represent the concerns expressed in non-state actor reports within Working Group proceedings (OHCHR 2021a). Non-state actors, in comparison, are restricted to observer status within Working Group meetings. To the extent that they may want to express themselves in the UPR process, they are only allowed to submit reports prior to Working Group sessions for potential inclusion in its "other stakeholders" report; delivering information to states participating in the Working Group meeting in hopes that they convey them in the Working Group deliberations; or issuing comments during the assembly of the Working Group outcome report (OHCHR 2021a). In essence, non-state actors are dependent upon the will of the Working Group and participating states to adopt the substance of their reports in evaluating a particular state.

Issues of access

Beyond the restrictions on participation in UPR Working Group proceedings, there were also antecedent challenges in the form of issues that impeded CIPM access to the UPR process. As described by Pwe-zay Y: "It's [the UPR] very technical and, on the other hand, very expensive and time consuming" (Interview Pwe-zay Y 2021). Such perception indicates several challenges with respect to (1) the gap between the knowledge and skills held by Myanmar indigenous CSOs versus the knowledge and skills tied to the workings of the UPR; (2) the gap between the financial resources of Myanmar indigenous CSOs versus the costs of travel to the site of the UPR, which during the time of fieldwork was conducted in-person in Geneva; and (3) the time available for Myanmar indigenous CSOs to devote to the UPR versus the time necessary to learn, prepare, and attend the UPR proceedings. In addition, interviews also noted that "In the collection of data, there were too many issues … so that it was also difficult selecting issues and tracking concrete primary sources" (Interview Pwe-zay Y 2021), suggesting that the scale of concerns among CIPM members made it difficult to organize themselves into a single coherent report for the UPR.

The formation of the CIPM itself as a coalition comprised of CSOs with an express purpose of engaging the UPR (OHCHR 2021c; CIPM 2020; HRC 2015) reflects the scale of effort necessary to overcome such challenges. The sentiment is reflected in a comment by Pwe-zay Y that "As a small local NGO organization, we can only submit a coalition report" (Interview Pwe-zay Y 2021), which suggests that the CIPM's formation was driven in some measure by a need for diverse local indigenous CSOs to pool their capacities. The process of alliance-building, however, was not entirely self-driven, in that members of the CIPM "joined a Burma UPR Forum … organized by Equality Myanmar" on making submissions to the UPR (Interview Pwe-zay Y 2021).

An entity founded and supported by the NGOs Equality Myanmar, Burma Partnership, and UPR Info Asia, the Burma UPR Forum (later Burma–Myanmar UPR Forum) operates with the purpose of preparing Myanmar CSOs for the UPR process and works with them to submit joint reports to the UPR Working Group sessions on Myanmar (see, for example, UPR Info Asia 2016; UPR Info Asia 2015; Burma–Myanmar UPR Forum 2015). All three NGOs are outside the membership of the CIPM and submitted UPR reports separately from the CIPM (CIPM 2020; HRC 2021c; HRC 2015), Hence, the involvement by members of CIPM in the Burma–Myanmar UPR Forum indicated their reliance upon non-indigenous entities for technical aid relevant for the UPR process. The issue of technical assistance went beyond the Burma–Myanmar UPR Forum, with an admission from Pwe-zay Y that "we had to hire a consultant for finalizing the [UPR] report" (Interview Pwe-zay Y 2021) pointing to the CIPM's need for additional expertise in preparing for the UPR.

Hence, in order to access the UPR process, Myanmar indigenous CSOs sought to ally themselves in a mutually supportive mission vis-à-vis the UPR. The CIPM represented an attempt to combine the capabilities and resources of Myanmar indigenous CSOs to address technical, financial, and time burdens entailed by the UPR process. But alliance formation as the CIPM was not enough, with the CIPM having to gain technical assistance from sympathetic actors in the form of NGOs and consultants with knowledge and skills relevant for the UPR. Such need poses a status of dependency, with Myanmar indigenous CSOs reliant upon the support of others in drafting their local indigenous concerns against the Myanmar state in a form acceptable to the international human rights mechanism of the UPR.

Issues of outcomes

As much as the CIPM worked to follow its commitment to engaging the UPR, the results of its efforts are somewhat mixed. Specifically, the limited nature of the UPR outcomes is apparent in the Myanmar state's deficiencies in fulfilling the Working Group outcome report recommendations—something recognized by Pwe-zay Y's observation that the UPR "is not legally binding and has not mandate" and as a result the Myanmar government "neglected most of the comments" in its outcome report (Interview Pwe-zay Y 2021). However, despite such dissatisfaction, there has been a measure of change in that Myanmar government "became more open for CSOs and NGOs in the discussion [of] legislation and launching projects," with new laws and policies "to ensure ... land ownership for local community" (Interview Pwe-zay Y 2021). In addition, specific to the issues of indigenous rights, interview comments also note that now "we can freely use the terms of indigenous peoples and many government staff acknowledge us as being indigenous people" and the government has issued laws and policies "which [have] given protection of land and forest, the use of Free Prior Informed Consent and traditional knowledge, etc." (Interview Pwe-zay Y 2021). It is not clear the CIPM's use of the UPR directly caused the aforementioned developments, but such comments indicate a perception of a link between them.

However, apart from a direct connection between UPR and the Myanmar state, there is an additional benefit in terms of broader exposure. Interview statements also observe that "There is no ... way to let the world know the human rights issues of a country and reviewing in one place" (Interview Pwe-zay Y 2021), reflecting a belief that the UPR provided value as a central forum drawing global attention to Myanmar's human rights problems. Such sentiments are bolstered by the activities of CIPM representatives via the distribution of fact sheets and holding of side events at the UPR site in Geneva, which indicate an ulterior view of the UPR as an opportunity to garner support from the delegates of the various states involved in Working Group proceedings (Interview Pwe-zay Y 2021).

CIPM's experiences display a measure of cautious optimism regarding the UPR, with views reflecting appreciation for its potential in terms of facilitating connections to sympathetic actors in the international community, qualified by a recognition of the anemic progress of the Myanmar state on human rights. The ambivalence is appropriate when considered against the orientation of UPR outcomes. Specifically, in evaluating the conduct of a given state, the UPR Working Group sessions work toward an outcome report whose contents summarize the information received about the state; questions, answers, and comments between the Working Group members and the state; findings of the Working Group; and recommendations for the state (OHCHR 2021a). As a result, the process is not judicial in terms of prescriptively rendering judgment and sanctions, but more instead descriptive in the sense of transcribing deliberations. While there is a prescriptive component in the form of outcome report recommendations, the focus is on connecting those recommendations to capacity-building and technical assistance efforts (OHCHR 2021a; Liljeblad 2018). In essence, the UPR does not seek to generate coercive measures to pressure states into improving their conduct on human rights but rather follows a collaborative orientation to improve a state's ability to meet UN human rights standards.

The nature of the UPR process aligns with theories of Constructivism in International Relations scholarship which favor norm-building through persuasion rather than confrontation, with international mechanisms wherein "actors are ideally arranged horizontally and all are empowered to contribute and shape discussion" with a depoliticized spirit of "free and open discussion between participants, who make recourse to the 'better' argument" (Davies 2010: 455). As much as the UPR Working Group sessions may encounter states that persistently violate human rights or resist the UPR process, the UPR mechanism adheres to a strategy of identifying state conduct that contravene human rights, urging problematic states to comply with international norms, and recording state behavior to inform considerations of non-compliance to UPR Working Group recommendations in the future (UNGA 2013).

To the extent that the UPR produces pressure upon a state, it comes through the transparency of UPR proceedings: all submissions and all outcome reports from Working Group sessions are publicly accessible, making it possible for any actor to use them as part of "naming and shaming" campaigns to mobilize public outrage pushing for international action against problematic states (Roth 2004). But such scenarios mean that the UPR is not directly conforming to the Boomerang Pattern model, in that pressure is coming from actors outside the UPR and not the UPR itself. In which case, the UPR's role vis-à-vis CIPM interests for pressure upon the Myanmar state is limited, with UPR processes working as an indirect conduit facilitating activism by others.

The preceding constraints pose a potential problem for Myanmar's indigenous peoples because they involve extended time frames. Any CIPM expectations to promote international pressure upon the Myanmar state must rely upon an indirect sequence of engaging the UPR mechanism, waiting for the UPR Working group to publish submissions and outcome reports, and looking for sympathetic international actors to then use such documents to mobilize a response. Even if CIPM expectations accept less confrontational results, the UPR's persuasive approach through capacity-building and technical assistance looks to norm-building that requires time extending beyond the more immediate complaints raised in CIPM's submissions. In short, by the time the UPR process results in behavioral change in the Myanmar state, there is a risk that Myanmar's indigenous communities will have already suffered irreversible damage to their environmental resources.

The issue of time is not purely speculative, with the Myanmar state displaying a lackluster response to the concerns of UPR outcome

reports. In particular, during the time of field study for the present analysis, the FIDH found that at the 2011 UPR Working Group session,
the Myanmar state accepted only 74 out of the 190 recommendations.
Even for the recommendations that it had accepted, the Myanmar state
failed to achieve a majority of them by 2015, despite enjoying several
years of international aid to do so (FIDH 2015).

Implications for theory

The efforts of the CIPM in relation to the UPR can be categorized
in terms of the ontology, epistemology, and resources tied to their
experiences identified in the preceding section regarding access, engagement, and outcomes from the UPR process. Ontological aspects arose
with respect to the UPR outcomes, with the CIPM's reflections indicating a recognition of the limits of the UPR power over the Myanmar
state even as it maintained a belief in the contributions of the UPR in
improving treatment of indigenous peoples within Myanmar and held
to aspirations of using the UPR as a way of exposing Myanmar indigenous complaints to an international audience. Such guarded perspective reflects an instrumentalist view of the UPR that is evocative of the
scholarship on bottom-up indigenous actions to use global institutions
to address local problems, particularly Vieira and Quack's work on
Brazilian indigenous use of the Catholic Church and international
NGOs (Vieira & Quack 2016), Saugestad's study on indigenous San
outreach to international NGOs (Saugestad 2011), or Xaxa's investigation on Indian indigenous connections to UN indigenous institutions
(Xaxa 2016). In taking an instrumentalist approach, the CIPM
exercised cross-issue linkages regarding indigenous identity, indigenous
claims to human rights, and indigenous concerns for the environment.
The linkages were apparent in the CIPM's submissions to the UPR,
which articulated indigenous and environmental grievances against the
Myanmar state within a vernacular of procedural rights and substantive rights available in international human rights law instruments. Such
efforts were successful, with the Working Group acceptance of CIPM's
submissions indicating its approval of the cross-issue linkages. CIPM's
approach aligns with scholarship on other indigenous movements which
have bridged the same slate of issues (see, for example, Belfer et al. 2019;
Pearl 2018; Mengden 2017; Noisecat 2016; Harry 2011; Anaya 2004b).
CIPM's experiences, however, add to the scholarship by demonstrating
the efficacy of cross-issue linkages with respect to the UPR, the HRC
as the body overseeing the UPR and its Working Group sessions, and
by extension the larger UN human rights system within which the HRC

functions. In doing so, it also complements the particular works of Vieira and Quack, Saugestad, and Xaxa by demonstrating the potential value in local indigenous movements reaching out to international human rights institutions.

Epistemological components involved the gaps between the members of CIPM and the UPR process in terms of the technical knowledge and skills required in (1) navigating the Working Group procedures and (2) phrasing Myanmar indigenous grievances regarding their environment as violations of human rights in a way that fell under the purview of Working Group's mandate. The difficulties encountered by indigenous groups in working with international mechanisms are a frequent topic in indigenous studies literature, particularly those centered around the contrasting worldviews and knowledge systems held by indigenous communities and international discourses (Liljeblad & Verschuuren 2019; Gombay & Palomino-Schalscha 2018; Escobar 2008). CIPM's case adds to such literature by identifying comparable issues with respect to the UPR, with CIPM's experiences indicating the significance of the gap between the base capacities of Myanmar's indigenous peoples and the necessary abilities associated with using the UPR process.

Resource components related to the aid provided by other NGOs and consultants which promoted capacity to achieve the above, with aid delivering knowledge, skills, and finances for the purpose of facilitating the coalescence of a united CIPM which could draw upon the collective resources of disparate member CSOs, empowering the CIPM to overcome the epistemological gaps in engaging the UPR, and endowing the CIPM with the ability to deliver its concerns to the Working Group sessions. The relationship between CIPM with NGOs and consultants follows the literature on sub-state indigenous activists who draw upon international aid providers to strengthen and expand their movements (Belfer et al. 2019; Martin 2011; Rodriguez-Garavito & Arenas 2005). The CIPM's experiences extend such literature to the space of the UPR, demonstrating the types of assistance needed from NGOs and consultants in connecting local indigenous struggles with a global human rights mechanism like the UPR.

Beyond the above components of scholarship, there is a larger significance from CIPM's exercise of the UPR arising from the totality of its experiences. Specifically, the breadth of CIPM efforts in relation to the UPR process raises implications for theory with respect to the sophistication of CIPM activities in linking multiple transnational strategies as instruments in a coordinated campaign. To begin, at a basic level, the CIPM's use of the UPR adhered to the Boomerang Pattern model of TANs, with the CIPM dealing with its domestic frustrations against the Myanmar state by reaching out to the UPR to generate international pressure to change the behavior of the Myanmar state. But CIPM engagement of the UPR involved a number of attendant steps that go beyond the basic form of the Boomerang Pattern: (1) coalition-building among disparate indigenous CSOs to from CIPM, (2) assistance by NGOs and consultants to render capacity-building aid, and (3) connection to attendees at Working Group sessions outside of session proceedings. First, coalition-building across Myanmar indigenous CSOs is more consistent with social movement theories, which recognize the possibilities for the formation of alliances across multiple CSOs for the purpose of escalating activism on shared causes (della Porta et al. 2006; della Porta & Tarrow 2004; Tarrow 2005; Khagram et al. 2002). To the extent that CSOs reflect social movements of people, the coalescence of the CIPM reflects an alliance of disparate Myanmar CSOs uniting to mobilize a common cause of indigenous rights. In addition, the position of NGOs and consultants in capacity-building more readily aligns with theories of intermediaries, which posit the notion of actors who connect local-level sub-state domestic discourses with global-level international discourses (Bettiza & Dionigi 2015; Golan & Orr 2012; Merry 2006). In endowing knowledge, skills, and finances to Myanmar indigenous CSOs, the NGOs and consultants which aided the formation and work of CIPM fulfilled an intermediary role in the sense that their activities helped domestic Myanmar indigenous CSOs connect to an international UPR process. Further, the connection to Working Group attendees at Working Group side events exemplifies the conceptualizations of social network theories that look to the construction of networks between actors which enable the exchange of information and resources (della Porta et al. 2006; Khagram et al. 2002). In hosting side events to distribute fact sheets and brief state delegates at the Working Group sessions, the CIPM built social networks with state representatives to convey information about Myanmar indigenous issues and nurture their support for Myanmar indigenous interests.

The outreach to state delegates in Working Group side events introduces a nuance to the application of network theories, particularly TANs, to the activities of the CIPM. The concept of TANs looks to common discourses of shared values mobilizing activism against states (Keck & Sikkink 1998). As a whole, the CIPM involvement with the UPR may have roughly followed the expectations of TANs, but there was a difference between the components of the network affiliated with the side events versus the components tied to the Working Group sessions. The side events facilitated direct communication with state delegates which opened more space for alliance-building with state actors with the potential to take action against the Myanmar, whereas the Working Group proceedings confined CIPM to observer positions unable to speak in Working Group sessions. As a result, the networks built in side events were more consistent with the notions of TANs, in that the side events provided a greater potential to foster a common discourse with state delegates in positions to mobilize actions by their respective states on behalf of indigenous issues in Myanmar. In contrast, CIPM involvement with the Working Group sessions was less likely to elicit such advocacy, since their distancing of CIPM meant less opportunity to directly connect in session discussions and hence less potential to direct session outcomes toward indigenous interests. The implication is that the networks formed with state delegates in side events were a subset of a larger network associated with the UPR, with the networks arising from the side events being more likely to function as TANs advocating for Myanmar indigenous interests while the larger network for the UPR was more inclined to function as a general network with weaker advocacy on Myanmar indigenous concerns.

The sum of the aforementioned body of phenomena is a broad ensemble of diverse strategies linked in a coordinated fashion to pursue a common endeavor of advancing Myanmar indigenous interests at a global level. The deployment of such a campaign differentiated a network into subsets, with one portion of the UPR network offering opportunities for more engagement with potential advocates and another portion restricting opportunities for mobilizing advocacy. The consequence is a more complex assembly of dynamics beyond the framework posed by the Boomerang Pattern model. Following the above analysis, the actors and interactions encompassing the CIPM, Myanmar state, and UPR mechanisms comprise a system illustrated in Figure 3.2.

To a degree, there is literature arguing that local indigenous groups can advance their interests by diversifying their activities to include alliances with sympathetic international actors, with particular advantages coming from international partners in non-indigenous issue spaces who are able to amplify indigenous causes to broader audiences (IWGIA 2011; Sawyer 2004; Gerlach 2003; Martin 2003; Wapner 1996). But the case of the CIPM with the UPR presents a demonstration of how diverse local sub-state indigenous CSOs can escalate their concerns to a global level not just through alliance formation with multiple international actors but also through a systematic campaign involving multiple transnational strategies that selectively used a specific subset of a larger network. The experiences of CIPM vis-à-vis the UPR indicate that the application of TANs theory was embedded in a wider suite of strategies encompassing nuanced exercise of social movement alliances,

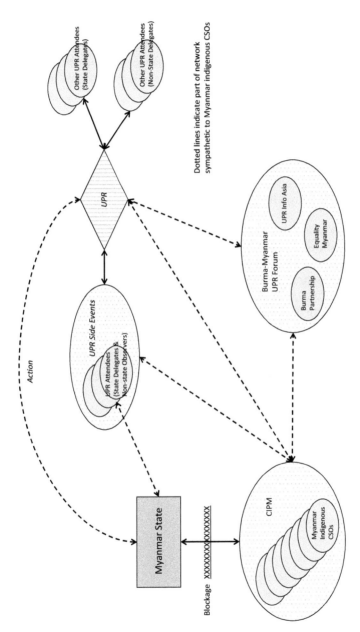

Figure 3.2 The Implications of the CIPM's Use of the UPR.

intermediaries, and social network theories. The CIPM's ability to focus such complexity in service of its mission to engage the UPR points to the potential value for indigenous peoples in the instrumental use of multiple coordinated strategies within a unified systematic campaign to advance particular goals.

Conclusion

In summary, the CIPM used the UPR as a vehicle to address the grievances of its member CSOs with the Myanmar state. In order to do so, it had to articulate indigenous concerns regarding the environment as forms of human rights issues in a way acceptable to the UPR Working Group session. Such work entailed an instrumental use of the UPR Working Group meetings to advance Myanmar indigenous complaints. Engagement with the UPR process, however, required an acquisition of knowledge, skills, and finances, which in turn incurred a need for aid from other NGOs and consultants. The sum of such issues called for sophistication terms of exercising multiple transnational strategies in a systematic campaign to elevate local Myanmar indigenous complaints to a global institution like the UPR. It should be noted that in focusing on the CIPM's use of the UPR, the analysis in the preceding sections dealt with a scenario where indigenous actors used an international human rights mechanism to address local environmental concerns. Chapter 4 turns to a situation of indigenous actors using an international environmental mechanism to address local human rights issues.

4 Myanmar Indigenous Engagement with the United Nations Framework Convention on Climate Change

The following sections complement Chapter 3 with an analysis of Myanmar indigenous activities vis-à-vis the 1992 United Nations Framework Convention on Climate Change (UNFCCC). While Chapter 3 investigated how indigenous actors sought to address local environmental problems by reaching out to an international human rights mechanism, the following sections explore how indigenous actors asserted their local concerns as human rights issues within an international environmental mechanism. The analysis looks to the work of Myanmar indigenous civil society organizations (CSOs) in engaging the UNFCCC system, identifying the issues that confronted their efforts and the consequent strategies they employed to overcome them.

Indigenous peoples are active in climate change discourses, with movements advancing indigenous concerns in state, regional, and global spaces (see, for example, Zentner et al. 2019; Canning 2018; Etchart 2017; McIntyre-Tamwoy et al. 2013; Doolittle 2010; Tsosie 2010; Heinamaki 2009; Gerrard 2008). The participation is motivated by the vulnerability of indigenous populations to climate change impacts, since many hold marginal status in terms of low socio-economic status, high dependency on local environments for sustenance, and general exclusion from decision-making processes that collectively leave them less resilient to ecosystem changes incurred by shifting climate patterns (Zentner et al. 2019; ILO 2017; Ford et al. 2016; Godden & Tehan 2016; Davis 2010). Indigenous activists assert the potential contributions of indigenous perspectives in larger efforts to counter climate change (Ford et al. 2016; Noisecat 2016; Tridgell 2016; Brewer & Warner 2015; Fernandez-Llamazares et al. 2015). To protect their rights, their welfare, and their perspectives, indigenous movements have sought to gain greater involvement in the deliberations of climate change fora such as the UNFCCC (Comberti et al. 2019; ILO 2017; Godden & Tehan 2016). While the state-centric nature of the UNFCCC has constrained

DOI: 10.4324/9781003133728-4

their opportunities for participation (Comberti et al. 2019; Havemann 2009), they have sustained efforts to secure more inclusion for indigenous voices within UNFCCC processes (Belfer et al. 2019; Ford et al. 2016; Doolittle 2010).

The mixture of indigenous issues and human rights in relation to climate change is possible under the UNFCCC (Powless 2012), with the Paris Agreement from the 21st Conference of the Parties (CoP) in 2015 asking state parties to include human rights and the rights of indigenous peoples among their obligations in addressing climate change (UNFCCC 2015: Preamble). Such sentiments extend to the UNFCCC system more broadly, with the report of the 16th CoP in 2010 recognizing a need to enable effective participation by indigenous peoples as stakeholders in climate change efforts at global, regional, national, and local levels (UNFCCC 2010: I(7)). Accompanying the acknowledgments of the UNFCCC are the activities of United Nations (UN) entities like the Office of the High Commissioner for Human Rights (OHCHR), which sustains an ongoing agenda to link human rights and climate change and advance human rights approaches in the formulation of climate change laws and policies (OHCHR 2021g), and the Human Rights Council (HRC), which in its Resolution 10/4 notes that climate change impacts threaten the enjoyment of human rights and that those impacts are greater for vulnerable populations such as indigenous peoples (HRC 2009). More recently, in July 2021, the HRC issued Resolution 47/24 calling upon the OHCHR and UN Secretary-General to produce reports on the harms incurred by climate upon vulnerable populations, including indigenous peoples, and the best practices in promoting and protecting their rights (HRC 2021b; OHCHR 2021h). As a result, the association of indigenous rights, human rights, and climate follows the reasoning of existing international UN programs, and to the extent that they relate to problems of climate change, human rights and indigenous issues fall under the purview of the UNFCCC.

The present analysis asserts that Myanmar indigenous approaches to the UNFCCC demonstrate abilities to exercise complex campaigns coordinating multiple transnational strategies spanning a spectrum of international actors to advance their interests in global, local, and substate spaces. While the outreach to the UNFCCC to address problems in Myanmar may suggest a direct action to bridge local issues and global mechanisms, the analysis seeks to identify deeper intricacies demonstrating a richer assembly of dynamics encompassing a wider array of interactions between diverse actors. The analysis begins with a review connecting theories of transnational advocacy networks (TANs) to the case of Myanmar indigenous peoples and the UNFCCC, along with a discussion of the methodology specific to the UNFCCC. The discussion then provides a background summarizing Myanmar's record under the UNFCCC and its treatment of indigenous peoples. The analysis continues with a presentation of findings regarding the struggles of Myanmar indigenous CSOs in utilizing the UNFCCC to address their grievances against the Myanmar state, after which the analysis generates implications for theories on transnational indigenous activism.

Theory and methodology

From a broad conceptual perspective, the involvement of Myanmar indigenous groups with the UNFCCC reflects another exercise of the "Boomerang Pattern" model applied in Chapter 3's analysis of the UN HRC Universal Periodic Review (UPR) mechanism. Specifically, following Margaret Keck and Kathryn Sikkink's prescriptions for the Boomerang Pattern (Keck & Sikkink 1998), Myanmar indigenous CSOs reached out to an international entity in the form of the UNFCCC to address issues related to local environments within Myanmar. In keeping with the precepts of the Boomerang Pattern and its associated larger literature on TANs, "international" indicates to the realm outside a single state's jurisdiction hosting interactions between and among state and non-state actors, and "local" or "domestic" refers to sub-state spaces under the jurisdiction of a single state (Keck & Sikkink 1998). Because Myanmar is a state party to the UNFCCC, the convention offers a potential means to influence Myanmar's conduct toward its indigenous peoples and their local environments. To the extent that their collective issues relate to a theme of climate change, the connection between the Myanmar state and Myanmar indigenous peoples through the UNFCCC adheres to the requirement of TANs for a network motivated by a "centrality of principles ideas or values" on climate change (Keck & Sikkink 1998: 1). Under the framework set by the UNFCCC in organizing global action to mitigate climate change, they also conform to the characteristics of TANs as comprised of actors working internationally who "are bound together by shared values, a common discourse, and dense exchange of information and services" (Keck & Sikkink 1998: 2). Following TAN theories, the promise of the UNFCCC is that it can collect and use data on climate change and actions to counter climate change to "persuade, pressure, and gain leverage" over state parties to alter their conduct (Keck & Sikkink 1998: 2).

Comparable to Chapter 3's discussion of the UPR, Myanmar indigenous use of the UNFCCC also reflects the trends of indigenous peoples under a state turning to strategies outside domestic borders, either transnationally to sympathetic allies in other states or internationally to global or regional mechanisms, to work against the intransigence of their state (Hochstetler & Keck 2007; Martin 2003). As such, it adds climate change as an issue space to the scholarship focused on TANs in cases linking indigenous rights, human rights, and environmental problems (Keck & Sikkink 1998). By extension, it also complements the wider scholarship on TANs involving indigenous rights more generally (Rodrigues 2004; Wright 2014).

In investigating the actions of Myanmar indigenous peoples vis-à-vis the UNFCCC, it is necessary to make several points in methodology beyond those given in Chapter 1. First, in exploring Myanmar indigenous engagement with the UNFCCC, the analysis employs a case study approach. In contrast to Chapter 3's study of the Coalition of Indigenous Peoples Myanmar (CIPM) with the UPR, for the UNFCCC there was no organized coalition of Myanmar indigenous CSOs comparable to the CIPM. As a result, the case is bounded in topic by the scope of the issues encompassed within the activities of Myanmar indigenous CSOs in the UNFCCC system and also bounded in time by the author's period of fieldwork 2015–2020. Second, the analysis draws upon primary and secondary source documents in the form of UNFCCC, Myanmar state, international nongovernmental organization (NGO), Myanmar indigenous CSO, and news media reports. In addition, the analysis gathers information from field notes and interviews conducted by the author, who served as a capacity-building consultant during that time to an individual Myanmar indigenous CSO involved in the UNFCCC. Third, the following sections follow the caution of Chapter 1 regarding the sensitivity of indigenous, human rights, and environmental issues, particularly with the escalation of conflict after the Myanmar military coup of February 2021 impacting all three issue spaces (EIA 2021a; EIA 2021b; OHCHR 2021f; Ong 2021). The use of field notes and interviews is complicated by the small number of Myanmar indigenous CSOs engaged with the UNFCCC during the identified time frame, which increases the risk for inference of identities even with the application of actions to anonymize sources, remove identifying information, and adhere to confidentiality. As a result, the analysis favors the use of publicly available materials in open circulation to avoid the risks of disclosing additional information and identities. Finally, in keeping with the observations in Chapter 1 regarding the fluid circumstances in Myanmar during the period of fieldwork, the analysis limits the scope of the case study to the activities of Myanmar indigenous CSOs within the framework of the UNFCCC system, such that the association with the UNFCCC constitutes a filter on the deliberations in the following sections.

Background

Myanmar is a state party to the UNFCCC, ratifying the convention in 1994 (UN 2021e; UN 2021f). It also ratified its subsequent Kyoto Protocol in 2003 and the Paris Agreement in 2017 (UNFCCC 2021). Myanmar's engagement with the UNFCCC and its attendant agreements is summarized by its National Determined Contributions 2021 Report (NDC Report), which identifies its adherence to the Paris Agreement with commitments to the Global Stocktake process; Greenhouse Gas (GHG) inventory reports; voluntary cooperation via international climate finance; strategies to increase forest carbon stocks; and institutions for monitoring, reporting, and verifications (MRV) requirements (IGES 2021; MoNREC 2021). The NDC Report builds upon a previous Intended National Determined Contributions 2015 Report (INDC Report), which constituted Myanmar's initial goals for carbon mitigation prior to the Paris Agreement 2016 (MoNREC 2015). The NDC Report built upon the INDC Report through a broad stakeholder consultation process that encouraged sectoral discussions during a preparatory phase lasting 2016–2018, a successive drafting phase in 2019–2020, and a finalization phase in the last quarter of 2020 (MoNREC 2021). The process to generate the NDC Report followed the Paris Agreement 2016, and in adherence to the country's commitments under the agreement presents a wide scope of agendas for carbon reductions involving reforms to energy, agriculture, forestry, transportation, and technology sectors (MoNREC 2021).

Associated with Myanmar's efforts vis-à-vis the UNFCCC is a broader array of climate change policies. On a national level, Myanmar has a Climate Change Policy 2018–2030, Climate Change Strategy 2018–2030, Climate Change Master Plan 2018–2030, and Sustainable Development Plan 2018–2030 (MoNREC 2019a; MoNREC 2019b; MoNREC 2019c). Parallel to the national-level statements are sectoral-specific policies that largely follow the NDC Report with corresponding supplementary climate change-related reforms, including the National Forestry Master Plan; Reforestation and Rehabilitation Program; National Electricity Master Plan; Waste Management Strategy and Master Plan; Hazardous Waste Management Master Plan; National Energy Efficiency and Conservation Policy, Strategy, and Roadmap; National Green Economy Policy Framework; National Environmental Strategic Framework and Master Plan; and Guidelines on Climate Change Resilient Architecture (IGES 2021; Liljeblad et al. 2021; MoNREC 2021).

The status of Myanmar's indigenous peoples within the above body of policies is tenuous. The more recent NDC Report includes mention of the terms "indigenous and community conservation areas" (ICCAs), "indigenous peoples," and "indigenous technology" (MoNREC 2021: xii–xiv). In addition, submissions to the UNFCCC Subsidiary Body for Scientific and Technological Advice (UNFCCC SBSTA) and the UNFCCC Standing Committee on Finance (UNFCCC SCF), respectively, reference indigenous knowledge systems and indigenous peoples (MoNREC 2020a; 2020b; UNFCCC STA 2016). Such inclusions, however, are general in the sense that they are policy documents and reports rather than declarations of law. Formal recognition in terms of legal authority is disputed. Specifically, Myanmar's 2008 Constitution follows the orientation of its 1982 Citizenship Law in identifying "national races" or "ethnic nationalities" and employs the term *"taing-yin-thar"* ("တိုင်းရင်းသား") to indicate groups present at the beginning of British annexation in 1823 Ethnic Rights Protection Law (ERPL) (CIPM 2015). The more recent ERPL 2015 contains the term *"htanay-taing-yin-thar"* ("ဌာနေတိုင်းရင်းသား"), but while some indigenous CSOs welcome this as describing indigenous peoples (CIPM 2015), the Myanmar state has interpreted this as denoting "local ethnic nationalities" (Morton 2017). A number of recent legislative acts, such as the Forest Law 2018 and Conservation of Biodiversity and Protected Areas Law 2018, avoid use of *htanay-taing-yin-thar* altogether (Liljeblad et al. 2021). The Myanmar indigenous CSOs involved with the UNFCCC also shared membership with the Coalition of Indigenous Peoples in Myanmar (CIPM), which suggests they held a conception of indigeneity that connected to the definition of *htanay-taing-yin-thar* raised in Chapter 3 of peoples having marginal status, continuous identity over time, ancestral territory, and self-determination.

The uncertainties extend to the functional aspects of Myanmar laws. To a degree, there are elements of Myanmar law that afford protections comparable to international legal instruments such as the UN Declaration on the Rights of Indigenous Peoples (UNDRIP) 2007. For example, the ERPL 2015 provides the right to free, prior, informed consent (FPIC) and right to language, both of which are in UNDRIP 2007 (ERPL 2015; UNDRIP 2007). Similarly, the National Land Use Policy (NLUP) 2016 addresses forms of shifting cultivation associated with notions of indigenous agriculture (NLUP 2016; POINT 2015; Progressive Voice 2018). But such recognition is countered by continuing practices of dispossession, with Myanmar indigenous activists arguing that instruments such as the Vacant, Fallow, and Virgin Lands Law 2012 and its 2018 Amendment have enabled seizure of lands lying predominately in indigenous areas and criminalized farming practices primarily practiced by indigenous peoples (Nyein 2020; Chau 2019; Progressive Voice 2018; VFV Amendment 2018; VFV Law 2012). The exercise of laws and policies with neutral language disproportionately harming indigenous peoples extends to Myanmar's efforts under the UNFCCC, with indigenous CSOs asserting that Myanmar's INDC Report 2015 proposed expansion of protected forest areas that took land and denied customary tenure practices of indigenous peoples (Myint 2017; POINT 2017). The more recent NDC Report 2021 asserts a need to improve collaboration with local and ethnic CSOs and contains terms such as "indigenous peoples," "indigenous and community conservation areas (ICCAs)," and "indigenous technology" but does not specify protections for indigenous rights or indigenous customary tenure systems (MoNREC 2021; IWGIA 2020a, 2020b; POINT 2020).

The need for more explicit provisions in Myanmar law for indigenous rights is heightened by the frustrations of indigenous peoples who have sought to defend their interests within the existing legal framework. For example, while the VFV Amendment 2018 recognized the notion of customary land tenure, it did not specify how to identify and register areas with customary land tenure systems (VFV Amendment 2018). As an additional example, Myanmar forestry management does not provide for FPIC, making it possible for the state to incorporate indigenous forests into state-controlled protected areas without need for consultation (CIPM 2020). Further, the entity formed to address land disputes, the Central Committee for Scrutinizing Confiscated Farmlands and Other Lands, does not have powers to return land, limiting the available remedies for indigenous complaints (CIPM 2020). Indigenous rights activists who have attempted to pursue legal actions have been subjected to harassment, arbitrary detentions, and enforced disappearances (HRC 2021c). Compounding the problems has been continuing broader discriminatory attacks on indigenous peoples, with persecution, violence, and denial of humanitarian aid by the military and state officials against indigenous communities (HRC 2021c).

In reaching out to the UNFCCC to address their issues with the Myanmar state, Myanmar indigenous CSOs conformed to the basic aspects of the Boomerang Pattern model presented by Keck and Sikkink. Confronted by continuing Myanmar state actions impairing their welfare, Myanmar indigenous activists sought recourse through UNFCCC mechanisms, essentially addressing local problems through actions accessing international avenues. Consistent with Keck and Sikkink's conception, the Myanmar indigenous CSOs who engaged the UNFCCC system adhered to a Boomerang Pattern working to generate

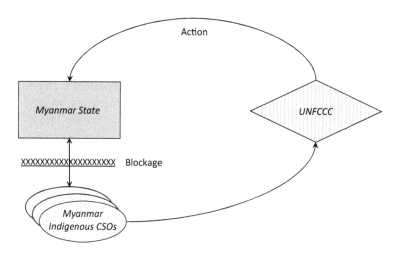

Figure 4.1 The "Boomerang Pattern" for Myanmar Indigenous CSOs with the UNFCCC.

transnational advocacy to alter the behavior of the Myanmar state. An illustration reflecting the Boomerang Pattern for Myanmar indigenous use of the UNFCCC is given by Figure 4.1.

Findings

The Myanmar indigenous CSOs who sought to participate in the UNFCCC followed a growing trend of engagement in UNFCCC mechanisms by non-state actors encompassing NGOs, corporations, international organizations, and media representing issues as diverse as agriculture, forestry, development, education, industry, law, religion, science, gender, youth, and indigenous peoples (Kuyper et al. 2018; Cabre 2011). To advance their respective interests within the UNFCCC, they exercise cross-issue linkages bridging their concerns to climate change. While limited in their roles relative to state parties in UNFCCC venues such as the CoPs, they use the UNFCCC as an opportunity space to influence state delegates and reach international audiences (Kuyper et al. 2018). Among other non-state actors, indigenous peoples have been able to participate in UNFCCC activities, elevating local issues of nature and culture to the global levels of the UNFCCC (Wani & Ariana 2018; NoiseCat 2016; Walbott 2014). Despite their efforts at agency, however, their impact within the UNFCCC system is constrained by institutional rules favoring states over non-state actors which operate to narrow the spaces for indigenous activism (Belfer et al. 2019; Comberti et al. 2019; Belfer et al. 2017).

Myanmar indigenous efforts vis-à-vis the UNFCCC reflect the above patterns, but a focus on their involvement provides details on the strategies they developed to overcome the difficulties of the UNFCCC. In turning to the UNFCCC to address their grievances, Myanmar indigenous peoples were challenged by the complexity of the UNFCCC system, which hosts an expansive assembly of instruments and institutions with different mandates and processes (UNFCCC Bodies 2021). In particular, the UNFCCC maintains bodies related to governance and process management, such as the annual CoPs and the Secretariat; subsidiary bodies fulfilling specific thematic issues, such as the SBSTA and Subsidiary Body for Implementation (SBI); constituted bodies formed by the CoPs, including the Adaptation Committee formed by the 16th CoP, SCF arising from the 16th CoP; Advisory Board of the Climate Technology Centre and Network (CTCN) created by the 18th CoP, and the Consultative Group of Experts (CGE) established by the 24th CoP (UNFCCC Bodies 2021). In addition are topic-specific processes, such as Reducing Emissions from Deforestation and Forest Degradation in Developing Countries (REDD+), which seeks to promote forests to increase carbon capture (UNFCCC REDD+ 2021a); and the Global Stocktake (GST) of the Paris Agreement to assess progress toward UNFCCC goals (UNFCCC GST 2021). Compared to such cases as the UPR, the breadth of UNFCCC components incurs a higher measure of demands upon potential participate with respect to awareness of each, knowledge and skills to navigate their respective procedures, and resources to engage their individual processes. The Myanmar state appears to have been able meet such demands, with UNFCCC records indicating that it has made submissions to multiple sessions of the CoPs, SBSTA, SCF, and REDD+ (UNFCCC Documents 2021; UNFCCC REDD+ 2021; UNFCCC Submissions 2021; MoNREC 2020a; MoNREC 2020b; UNFCCC REDD+ 2019). However, it is less clear if Myanmar indigenous peoples lacking the capacities of the state have also been able to overcome such requirements.

Determination of Myanmar indigenous capacities to advance their interests vis-à-vis the UNFCCC requires navigation through the intricacies of the UNFCCC system, with its array of potential venues for engagement increasing the difficulties of compiling submissions reflecting Myanmar indigenous complaints. But a measure of illustrative evidence is available in the form of reports submitted to UNFCCC mechanisms by the Asia Indigenous Peoples Pact (AIPP) and International Work

Group in Indigenous Affairs (IWGIA), both of which are NGOs allied with Myanmar indigenous CSOs (see, for example, AIPP 2020; IWGIA 2019a; IWGIA 2019b; AIPP 2017a). While they do not constitute a comprehensive body of all issues raised by Myanmar indigenous peoples to the UNFCCC, they are sufficient to serve the purpose of demonstrating the association of Myanmar indigenous grievances and human rights issues within UNFCCC venues.

To begin, in joint and separate reports, both organizations called for greater inclusion of Myanmar's indigenous peoples in Myanmar's climate change policies and greater participation in decision-making systems (AIPP 2020; IWGIA 2019a; IWGIA 2019b). Such a call incurred the right to participation, which is expressed by international human rights instruments such as Articles 5, 18, 19, and 27 of the 2007 UNDRIP (UNDRIP 2007: Arts. 5, 18, 19, 27) and complemented by the right to participate in public affairs given by instruments such as Article 21 of the 1948 Universal Declaration of Human Rights (UDHR) and Article 25 of the 1966 International Covenant on Civil and Political Rights (ICCPR) (ICCPR 1966: Art. 25; UDHR 1948: Art. 21). The IWGIA combined the expectation for inclusion with a call for elimination of discrimination based on factors such as gender, ethnicity, age, or disability (IWGIA 2019a; IWGIA 2019b), which is aligned with provisions on equity and nondiscrimination exemplified by Articles 1–6 and 22 of UNDRIP (UNDRIP 2007: Arts. 1–6, 22); Article 2 of the UDHR (UDHR 1948: Art. 2); Articles 2, 3, 14, 24, 26, and 27 of the ICCPR (ICCPR 1966: Arts. 2–3, 14, 24, and 26–27), and Articles 2 and 3 of the 1966 International Covenant on Economic, Social, and Cultural Rights (ICESCR) (ICESCR 1966: Arts. 2 and 3). In addition, reports from both the AIPP and IWGIA identified the rights of Myanmar indigenous peoples to land and forms of customary land tenure (AIPP 2020; IWGIA 2019a; IWGIA 2019b), which aligned with rights to land expressed in such instruments as Articles 10 and 24–30 of UNDRIP and Article 15 of the ICESCR (UNDRIP 2007: Arts. 10 and 24–30; ICESCR 1966: Art. 15). Further, both organizations asserted the need for FPIC, which is contained in Articles 10, 11, 19, 24, 31, and 32 of UNDRIP (UNDRIP 2007: Arts. 10, 11, 19, 23, 31, and 32). Moreover, IWGIA reports involving Myanmar indigenous peoples also raised the need to ensure living in a healthy environment with fair and sustainable development (IWGIA 2019a; IWGIA 2019b), which tied to the right to a healthy environment in Article 29 and the right to sustainable development in Articles 23 and 32 of UNDRIP (UNDRIP 2007: Arts. 23, 29, and 32). Last, the IWGIA asserted the ability of indigenous peoples to form their own conservation areas and attendant governance models without recognition of government (IWGIA 2019a), connoting the right to self-determination contained in such instruments as Article 3 of UNDRIP; Article 1 of the ICCPR, and Article 1 of the ICESCR (UNDRIP 2007: Art. 3; ICCPR 1966: Art. 1; ICESCR 1966: Art. 1). In their respective reports, the AIPP and IWGIA did not specifically identify what arguments tied to which corresponding articles in international human rights instruments, but in a joint report referencing Myanmar indigenous peoples, they indicated an association between the two by observing the 2015 Paris Agreement Preamble's admonition "to respect human rights and the rights of indigenous peoples when taking action to address climate change" (AIPP 2020).

The expression of Myanmar indigenous concerns via proxies like the AIPP and IWGIA was driven by issues in the UNFCCC that obstructed the involvement of Myanmar indigenous CSOs. In particular, the nature of the UNFCCC system posed challenges affecting engagement in terms of constraints upon the activities indigenous CSOs could undertake as non-state actors in a state-centric structure, access in terms of the work required by indigenous actors in reaching out to UNFCCC mechanisms, and outcomes in terms of the subsequent results affecting indigenous interests from the UNFCCC. Each category of issues is addressed in the respective subsections below.

Issues of engagement

With respect to engagement, Myanmar indigenous peoples encountered restrictions arising from the state-centric nature of the processes under the convention. The UNFCCC distinguishes between state and non-state participants. State parties are classified into Non-Annex I, which encompasses developing countries accorded special considerations in aid due to their limited capacity and high vulnerability to climate change; Annex I, which refers to economies-in-transition deserving of some assistance; and Annex II, which identifies industrialized countries given full duties to reduce carbon emissions and render aid to Annex I and Non-Annex I states (UNFCCC Stakeholders 2021). Despite the differences, all state parties enjoy the same basic privileges of making submissions or participating in the deliberations of UNFCCC-affiliated bodies (UNFCCC Stakeholders 2021). All other entities, including non-party observer states, international governmental organizations (IGOs), and NGOs, are limited to observer status, which allows submissions of reports to participants at UNFCCC-related proceedings but denies engagement within those proceedings (UNFCCC Stakeholders 2021; UNFCCC Submissions 2021).

The category of observers, however, is not open, in that the UNFCCC holds a further constraint of requiring admission to observer status, effectively narrowing the space for non-state entities allowed to make submissions or attend UNFCCC events (UNFCCC Observers 2021). Without admission to observer status, non-state actors are treated as constituencies or informal groups that are barred from UNFCCC-related proceedings and relegated to either hosting side events or working through admitted observers (UNFCCC Admitted NGOs 2021). Indigenous NGOs who are not admitted to observer status are treated as a constituency and have two venues in which they can act: the International Indigenous Peoples' Forum on Climate Change (IIPFCC), which is a caucus to help coordinate indigenous interests and generate specific indigenous points for discussion within UNFCCC processes (IIPFCC 2021), and the Local Communities and Indigenous Peoples Platform (LCIPP), which is a working group for indigenous peoples to inform UNFCCC policies and practices on indigenous issues (LCIPP 2021). Neither space offers power equivalent to states in UNFCCC governing and management bodies like the CoP, functioning instead more as coordinating, communicating, and consultative components for indigenous issues within the UNFCCC system (IIPFCC 2021; LCIPP 2021). As of 2021, there were no Myanmar indigenous CSOs on the list of NGOs admitted to observer status, and the only indigenous NGO from Asia having observer status was the AIPP (UNFCCC Admitted NGOs 2021). Such conditions left Myanmar indigenous groups with limited options for engaging the UNFCCC system: organize side events, work through proxies admitted to observer status like the AIPP, or participate in constituency venues such as the IIPFCC and LCIPP.

Issues of access

While the state-centric nature of the UNFCCC may have reduced the available spaces for action by Myanmar indigenous CSOs, it did not entail a correlating amelioration of difficulties in connecting to those spaces. For example, a joint AIPP–IWGIA report submitted to the UNFCCC encompassing Myanmar indigenous CSOs noted issues of access regarding lack of capacity in financial resources and technical knowledge and skills required to engage the limited available spaces for participation in the UNFCCC system (AIPP 2020). The inclusion of Myanmar indigenous peoples in the AIPP and IWGIA report suggests some measure of their attendant involvement with UNFCCC activities, but discernment of the scope and details of involvement is not as straightforward as the case of the UPR, in that there was no identifiable coalition of Myanmar indigenous CSOs for the UNFCCC fulfilling a role comparable to that of the CIPM with the UPR. Instead, reference to primary source documents held by UNFCCC-related entities such as the SBSTA, LCIPP, and UN-REDD Programs, in combination with public accessible announcements from NGOs and news media regarding UNFCCC-related events, present a scenario of disparate Myanmar indigenous CSOs exercising different avenues to connect to the UNFCCC system at global, regional, and national levels.

To begin, global-level strategies involved outreach to central multilateral UNFCCC processes held by its annual CoPs, subsidiary bodies, and constituency bodies. Without admitted observer status, Myanmar indigenous CSOs could not attend the proceedings of the CoPs or subsidiary bodies. They were, however, able to find alternative means for action by working with sympathetic multinational organizations holding admitted observer status such as the AIPP, which includes Myanmar indigenous CSOs among its multinational member organizations (AIPP 2021), and the IWGIA, which identifies both the AIPP and Myanmar indigenous CSOs within its list of international partners (IWGIA 2021b; UNFCCC Stakeholders 2021). In particular, records for the CoPs show a consistent attendance by AIPP, working with entities such as the Center for International Forestry Research (CIFOR), IWGIA, and Nepal Federation of Indigenous Nationalities (NFIN) for the more recent 2017 CoP 23 in Bonn, Germany (AIPP 2017a; AIPP 2017b; CIFOR 2017; DOCIP 2021); 2018 CoP 24 in Katowice, Poland (LCIPP 2019b); and 2021 CoP 26 in Glasgow, Scotland (IWGIA 2020b; UNFCCC SEORS 2021). AIPP also facilitated engagement with UNFCCC subsidiary bodies outside the CoPs, with the example of its contributions as a non-party stakeholder to the 50th Session of the SBSTA held in 2019 in Bonn, Germany (UNFCCC 2019a; UNFCCC STA 2019a). The AIPP continued its facilitative role for events held by the UNFCCC constituency bodies IIPFCC and LCIPP, both in terms of participating in their individual meetings or in conjunction with their side events at other UNFCCC body proceedings (see, for example, AIPP 2020; IWGIA 2020a; LCIPP 2019a; LCIPP 2019b; UNFCCC STA 2019b). In representing the interests of its member organizations across the aforementioned range of events, the AIPP effectively functioned as a proxy for Myanmar indigenous CSOs, allowing them indirect means of involvement with the global-level proceedings of UNFCCC bodies.

In addition to global strategies, there were more regional and sub-state strategies for action. Regional strategies involved mechanisms aimed at actors within Asia vis-à-vis the larger UNFCCC system. Examples involving Myanmar indigenous CSOs include conferences hosted by

AIPP for Asian indigenous organizations, with examples including a 2015 workshop in Thailand to develop common thematic discussion points across Asian indigenous groups for the CoP 21 in Paris, France (AIPP 2015), and another 2019 workshop on indigenous women aimed at consolidating a unified message for the CoP 25 in Madrid, Spain (Cuso 2019). Sub-state actions encompass domestic events associated with global UNFCCC processes. Examples for Myanmar are consultation workshops for REDD+ organized at different times by the Myanmar state, UN-REDD Program, and AIPP that welcomed the participation of Myanmar indigenous CSOs to advance their concerns with Myanmar's forestry plans (UN REDD 2021; UN REDD 2020; UN REDD 2016).

But entities like AIPP do not function alone, in that they worked in conjunction with other NGOs such as the CIFOR, Cuso International, the IWGIA, and NFIN, meaning that there was a network of allied NGOs collaborating in indigenous-related events at various UNFCCC proceedings. Each NGO, however, was in turn dependent upon additional actors in the form of aid providers who rendered financial and technical support. For example, AIPP work on climate change is funded by the Norway's International Climate and Forest Initiative (NICFI) (AIPP 2020). Similarly, the IWGIA's climate change agenda is funded by NICFI and the Danish International Development Agency (DANIDA) (AIPP 2020). CIFOR draws upon financial and technical assistance from a range of multilateral, state, and non-state sources, including the Austrian Development Agency (ADA), European Commission, Food and Agriculture Organization (FAO), Global Environment Facility (GEF), International Land Coalition (ILN), Norwegian Agency for Development and Cooperation (NORAD), Swedish International Development Cooperation Agency (SIDA), United Nations Development Programme (UNDP), United States Agency for International Development (USAID), World Bank (CIFOR 2021), and a host of universities around the world (CIFOR 2021). Cuso International donors include the European Union, Global Affairs Canada, United Nations Refugee Agency, and the World Food Program (Cuso 2021).

The consequence is that access for Myanmar indigenous CSOs to the UNFCCC system was enabled by a deep network of NGOs, multilateral institutions, and state and private sector donors. While they may not have explicitly directed aid toward Myanmar indigenous CSOs, their agendas did look to climate change issues and by extension the disparate components of the UNFCCC. To the extent that their activities allied with the concerns of indigenous peoples regarding climate change, they opened a collective body of financial and technical resources available for indigenous organizations seeking to engage UNFCCC processes. In specific relation to the UNFCCC, such aid went largely to entities admitted to observer status like the AIPP and IWGIA, but their inclusion of Myanmar indigenous CSOs rendered them as conduits for financial and technical aid that elevated Myanmar indigenous concerns to the global-level mechanisms of the UNFCCC.

Such issues raise a potential position of dependency, with Myanmar indigenous activists relying upon the discretion of partners to act as proxy representatives advancing Myanmar indigenous interests within various UNFCCC venues and as aid providers facilitating Myanmar indigenous capacities to contribute to UNFCCC events. Bereft of partner commitment, Myanmar indigenous groups would have been left with limited resources and little avenues of access to the UNFCCC system. As a result, the presence of Myanmar indigenous CSOs within the UNFCCC was a function of their abilities to form alliances with sympathetic actors having access to UNFCCC mechanisms and willing to use such access on behalf of Myanmar indigenous concerns.

Issues of outcomes

Last, with respect to outcomes, it is not clear that the efforts to use the UNFCCC pushed the Myanmar state to alter its treatment of indigenous peoples or address their concerns regarding the environment. On a general level, the powers for compliance under the UNFCCC are somewhat ambiguous, with the nature of enforcement differing for disparate UNFCCC climate change agreements. For example, the Kyoto Protocol provides for a Compliance Committee with the mandate to impose consequences for state party failure to meet the protocol's commitments, but the consequences involve identification of state noncompliance, analysis for the reasons of noncompliance, suspension from the protocol, or adjustments in a state's allocation of emissions (UNFCCC 2005). In contrast, the Paris Agreement specifies that its Compliance Committee is "facilitative in nature and function in a manner that is transparent, non-adversarial, and non-punitive" (UNFCCC 2019b: 60). As a result, the tenor of the UNFCCC system is that state compliance is largely voluntary, with limited pressure to compel changes in state behavior on any issues under the UNFCCC. The consequence is that as much as there may be sympathy among actors participating in the spaces of the UNFCCC, it is not clear that there is any assurance of action that can force states to address indigenous issues.

Admittedly, there have been some signs of increasing Myanmar state receptiveness to indigenous interests, with Myanmar's 2021 NDC Report mentioning the terms "indigenous peoples," "indigenous and community conservation areas (ICCAs)," and "indigenous technology" (MoNREC 2021); Myanmar's 2020 proposal for input to the UNFCCC SCF using the term "indigenous people" and "indigenous and local knowledge" (MoNREC 2020a); and Myanmar's 2016 submission to the Addendum to the UNFCCC SBSTA Advice 44 applying the term "indigenous knowledge systems" (UNFCCC STA 2016). However, such developments did not necessarily arise as a result of Myanmar indigenous CSOs engaging with the UNFCCC system and could be motivated by reasons unrelated to UNFCCC-related indigenous activities.

In addition, the exercises of the aforementioned concepts within UNFCCC-related Myanmar state documents do not assure enforcement through legal authorities, in that they are documents on policies rather than declarations of law. They may serve the requirements of meeting legal obligations of Myanmar as a state party to the UNFCCC as an international legal instrument, but individually they do not represent legal instruments comparable to the status of legislative acts or court decisions in domestic law. Hence, without the formality of expression in law, they reflect informal acknowledgments of concepts regarding indigenous issues within a confined context of UNFCCC reporting requirements.

A potential mitigating factor is the UNFCCC's recognition of indigenous issues. In addition to the functions of the IIPFCC and LCIPP, there has been a statement by the 2016 Paris Agreement that instructs state parties to "respect, promote, and consider their respective obligations on human rights," including "the rights of indigenous peoples" when taking action on climate change (Boyle 2018: 769–770; UN 2015: Preamble). The UNFCCC does not require transparency on each state party's performance on human rights, even as it does so for their progress on climate change (Duyck et al. 2018), but the HRC has argued that there is a duty for state parties under the UNFCCC to assure respect for human rights (HRC 2016). As a result, there is a call upon the Myanmar state as a state party to the UNFCCC to meet its aspirations for addressing human rights claims of Myanmar indigenous peoples. But the presence of such an expectation does not affirm a direct connection between Myanmar indigenous activism in the UNFCCC and the conduct of the Myanmar state toward its indigenous populations.

The limitations of the UNFCCC were acknowledged by a representative of a Myanmar indigenous CSO, Pwe-zay Z, who in discussing the impact of their work with the UNFCCC upon the Myanmar state observed that "there were changes and improvement in law and policy but it will not be directly related as a result of our participation in UNFCCC" (Interview Pwe-zay Z 2021). The utility of the UNFCCC, however, may go beyond outcomes in laws or policies in the sense that the effort of access and engaging the UNFCCC itself entails an elevation of Myanmar indigenous issues into national, regional, and global spaces that may reach wider audiences. Such amplification of awareness may mark Myanmar indigenous concerns as significant and hence deserving of attention. The value of attention is reflected by Pwe-zay Z in describing the benefit of the UNFCCC system as "its accreditation, we got acknowledgement or respect while attending national and regional consultation workshop[s] and our discussion[s] are taken into account by government representatives" (Interview Pwe-zay Z 2021). The extent of the resulting impact was apparently tentative, with the interview also noting that "many government staffs recognized and acknowledged that indigenous peoples are protector of forest and slightly open up the participation of indigenous peoples in the process of formation and consultation" (Interview Pwe-zay Z 2021). But the aforementioned sentiments indicate a measure of value from the exposure offered by the UNFCCC system in nurturing more receptivity to Myanmar indigenous interests, with the recognition by the UNFCCC of indigenous rights and human rights opening spaces for indigenous perspectives as an integral topic in UNFCCC-related discourses—spaces which host engagement by state parties such as Myanmar. In which case, the utility of the UNFCCC for Myanmar indigenous peoples depends on the expectations for its outcomes. To the extent that aspirations seek direct consequences in the formal instruments of the Myanmar state, the effectiveness of the UNFCCC may be ambiguous, but to the extent that hopes look to alterations in perceptions and attendant behavior by the Myanmar state, the UNFCCC may provide more assistance.

Implications for theory

The preceding sections present several observations on Myanmar indigenous experiences with the UNFCCC system that roughly parallel the ontological, epistemological, and resource-related comments regarding Myanmar indigenous use of the UPR. With respect to ontology, there was a measure of ambivalence in the UNFCCC outcomes, with the appearance of concepts regarding indigenous peoples and indigenous rights in Myanmar's UNFCCC submissions—as illustrated by the 2021 NDC Report, 2020 SCF proposal, and 2016 STA addendum—constituting only informal actions that lacked the formal substance of expression in Myanmar laws. To a degree, the absence of legal expression was mitigated by a functional increase in acceptance of indigenous representation by Myanmar state officials in consultation processes for law and policy. But it was not clear that the improvements in indigenous status under the Myanmar state were a result of UNFCCC activities. Despite the uncertainty, following from Pwe-zay Z's interview, there was at least one CSO which believed the effort to participate in global-level UNFCCC mechanisms facilitated respect from Myanmar state representatives at regional and sub-state UNFCCC-related events. Hence, similar to the assessment of Myanmar indigenous engagement with the UPR, Myanmar indigenous involvement in the UNFCCC system can be characterized as guarded, with mixed assurances as to its value in fulfilling Boomerang Pattern expectations of pressure altering Myanmar state behavior.

In regard to epistemology, there was a parallel in the knowledge and skills gaps between Myanmar indigenous experiences with the UPR and UNFCCC, respectively. Just as much as the UPR mechanism posed technical challenges in terms of institutionally specific practices, the UNFCCC system also entailed technical issues that challenged Myanmar indigenous CSOs. The difference, however, was that the UNFCCC hosted a much broader scale encompassing multiple venues spanning global, regional, and sub-state scales exercising different practices. As a result, relative to the UPR, navigating the intricacies of the UNFCCC to find paths for Myanmar indigenous engagement required a higher order of capabilities.

With respect to resources, for both cases of UPR and UNFCCC, there is also rough similarity in the dependence by Myanmar indigenous groups upon assistance from sympathetic international actors. Similar to the UPR, in the case of the UNFCCC, Myanmar indigenous CSOs received financial resources and technical knowledge and skills from international NGOs like the AIPP. There is a difference, however, in that finances, knowledge, and skills were not enough for engagement with the UNFCCC system, since the UNFCCC rules on participation by non-state actors also meant that Myanmar indigenous groups were dependent upon organizations with observer status like the AIPP to advance their interests within UNFCCC mechanisms. Hence, Myanmar indigenous groups needed not only capacity-building services but also proxy representation from partners with greater abilities, familiarity, and privileges within the UNFCCC system. In addition, there is also another difference in that organizations like the AIPP themselves were further aided by other entities, meaning that Myanmar indigenous groups were benefiting not from a single partner for help but rather a network of multiple aid providers associated with the UNFCCC. While not all the members of the network shared a specific interest in indigenous or Myanmar issues, they did share sufficiently common interests regarding climate change that were expansive enough to encompass the concerns of Myanmar indigenous peoples within their aid activities. In essence, to the extent that could phrase indigenous concerns for the environment as climate change problems, Myanmar indigenous groups benefited from having their agendas embedded within the ensemble of agendas held by a transnational network of actors working together for a larger cause of climate change.

The struggles of Myanmar indigenous groups with the complexities of the UNFCCC system generate larger implications for theory that differ from those displayed with the UPR. On a conceptual level, there is consistency with the general model of the Boomerang Pattern of TANs in the endeavor of indigenous peoples in Myanmar addressing their grievances by reaching outside Myanmar for help from the international community. But Myanmar indigenous activities in relation to the UNFCCC did not follow the dynamics displayed with the UPR. First, for the UPR Myanmar indigenous CSOs worked to form a coalition in the CIPM, gained capacity-building assistance from intermediary NGOs and consultants, and then pursued networks to reach Working Group sessions and the state delegates attending those session. In comparison, for the UNFCCC, there was no coalition and disparate Myanmar indigenous CSOs had to partner with international actors with access and capacity to engage UNFCCC processes. Selection of the partners was specific, in that in order to facilitate Myanmar indigenous voices within UNFCCC spaces they had to be entities admitted to observer status, and hence allowed to observe the proceedings of UNFCCC mechanisms and engage their accompanying side events, with the financial resources and technical knowledge and skills requisite for participation in each.

Second, such partners were not alone but were in turn connected to other allied actors sharing agendas vis-à-vis the UNFCCC. The consequence was that Myanmar indigenous concerns for the environment were incorporated into a slate of compatible issues under a common umbrella of climate change. To the extent that the assembly was international, it fulfilled the parameters of TANs in the sense of reflecting a transnational network of actors with aligned interests oriented toward a common discourse tied to the UNFCCC (Keck & Sikkink 1998). The complexities of the UNFCCC system, however, meant that such a TAN did not engage the UNFCCC as a unitary entity but rather worked through the UNFCCC's disparate components for observer engagement, with various activities connecting to a range of UNFCCC mechanisms at global, regional, and sub-state levels. In essence, it was a transnational network advocating a slate of agendas through a corresponding transnational network of UNFCCC-related processes spanning multiple levels.

Last, the network of entities sympathetic to Myanmar indigenous interests was only a subset of a larger network of actors associated with the UNFCCC. The UNFCCC system connects to a global network of state and non-state actors that may share a common nexus on the topic of climate change but otherwise can diverge in their respective agendas. Hence, as much as Myanmar indigenous activists found support from a segment of the UNFCCC network encompassing the AIPP, its allies, and their attendant donors, the UNFCCC network also hosts other portions with actors and donors that are not necessarily sympathetic or cognizant of Myanmar indigenous interests or indigenous issues in general. In essence, the UNFCCC network hosts diverse subnetworks with different ensembles of actors whose interests are not always compatible with each other. The consequence is that while the collection of Myanmar indigenous CSOs, the AIPP, and its associated allies and donors may have comprised a TAN supportive of Myanmar indigenous interests, it was subsumed within a larger UNFCCC network that also hosted other subnetworks with unclear positions on the interests of Myanmar indigenous peoples.

The above observations identify the ways in which Myanmar indigenous exercise of the UNFCCC went beyond the conceptions of a Boomerang Pattern model. While Myanmar indigenous CSOs used the UNFCCC as an international means to address local grievances against the Myanmar state, their efforts exhibited more complex connections to multiple venues with transnational networks connecting different actors and issues. Within such spaces, the conduct of the Myanmar state against Myanmar indigenous peoples became only one topic among many. To the extent, however, that any topic connected to climate change, it aided Myanmar indigenous interests by amplifying their concerns to a wider audience of sympathetic actors in the international community. The nature of the networks for Myanmar indigenous CSOs vis-à-vis the UNFCCC system is represented by Figure 4.2.

The end result of the above dynamics aligns with that observed for Myanmar indigenous peoples and the UPR: the association with sympathetic international actors through a systematic application of multiple transnational strategies can amplify originally local concerns to a global level. In addition, the above observations evoke the case of the UPR in terms of Myanmar indigenous CSOs finding and using TANs

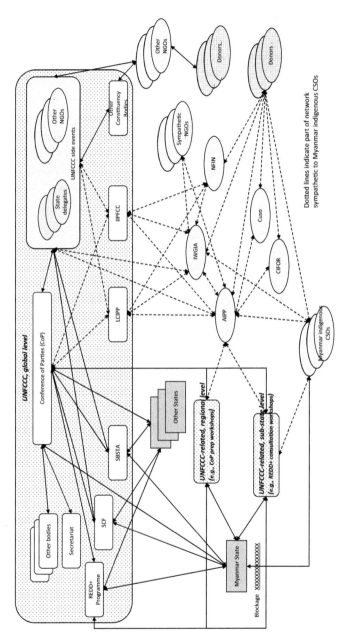

Figure 4.2 The Implications of Myanmar Indigenous Use of the UNFCCC.

that are subsets within larger networks associated with the operations of an international mechanism. But whereas the collection of strategies for the UPR encompassed social movement alliances, intermediaries, and social networks around a single mechanism, for the UNFCCC, the suite of strategies relates more to a larger meaning of networks encompassing social networks of various supporters engaging with venue networks of diverse UNFCCC mechanisms on different issues networked around a theme of climate change. The sophistication exhibited in exercising campaigns with the above qualities reflects the capacities of Myanmar indigenous activists and suggests a potential utility for indigenous peoples more generally with respect to similar approaches toward other networks in alternative issue spaces.

Conclusion

To finish, the preceding sections delineated how Myanmar indigenous CSOs managed to advance their interests within the UNFCCC system, linking indigenous local grievances against the Myanmar state as human rights issues with the scope of UNFCCC agendas on climate change. The nature of the UNFCCC system required that Myanmar indigenous CSOs overcome issues challenging their involvement through the exercise of multiple strategies with diverse allies spanning global, regional, and sub-state mechanisms in the UNFCCC system. Such activities build upon the sophistication of Myanmar indigenous engagement with the UPR previously studied in Chapter 3, with the present chapter indicating additional capacities by Myanmar indigenous CSOs for more expansive campaigns extending through networks encompassing layers of interlinked social actors, venue spaces, and issues.

5 Conclusion
Implications and Directions for Future Research

The present chapter concludes the collective work of preceding ones by drawing broader implications for more generalizable theory. Specifically, the following sections identify how the experiences of Myanmar indigenous civil society organizations (CSOs) with the Universal Periodic Review (UPR) and United Nations Framework Convention on Climate Change (UNFCCC) add detail to understandings of indigenous peoples agency that complement elements in the fields of International Relations and International Law. The discussion finishes with a comment on directions for future research.

International relations

The work of the previous chapters complements scholarship in the field of International Relations with details on the nature of indigenous agency in the structure of international discourses on human rights and environment. In exploring the substance of agency expressed by Myanmar indigenous groups, the analyses in the chapters delineated the strategies exercised by Myanmar indigenous activists in bringing local issues to international mechanisms. For the UPR, Myanmar indigenous CSOs combined intermediaries and social movement alliances encompassed in broader social networks which spanned local and global discourses and linked indigenous concerns for environmental harms to human rights issues. For the UNFCCC, Myanmar indigenous CSOs also blended intermediaries, social movement alliances, and social networks, but with additional dimensions of linking multiple mechanisms within the UNFCCC system at local, regional, and global levels with a broader range of actors with a wider range of cross-issue linkages to climate change. The central thematic element across both cases is networking, in that for both the UPR and UNFCCC Myanmar peoples followed

DOI: 10.4324/9781003133728-5

avenues for indigenous identity to join transnational networks of sympathetic actors offering aid. The experiences of Myanmar indigenous peoples in the UPR and UNFCCC present permutations of such transnational networks, with each involving different ways of relating local indigenous issues to international human rights and international environmental principles amenable to the attention of corresponding global mechanisms. The aforementioned qualities indicate a multifaceted sophistication in formulating multi-strategy, multi-actor, multi-issue approaches specific to individual global mechanisms, with the goal of making instrumental use of each to address domestic grievances against the Myanmar state.

The nature of agency through networks becomes more significant when viewed in relation to the structural constraints presented by the UPR and UNFCCC. The UPR privileges United Nations (UN) member states in its Working Group sessions, marginalizing non-state actors such as indigenous peoples to limited roles in submitting reports, observing proceedings, or conducting side events (Higgins 2019; Higgins 2014). Similarly, the UNFCCC places state parties at a primary level in a hierarchy, with state parties enjoying participation in UNFCCC mechanisms and indigenous groups largely left to non-state activities of providing submissions, witnessing events, or joining side events and constituency forums (Belfer et al. 2019; Cabre 2011; Comberti et al. 2019; Kuyper et al. 2018; Belfer et al. 2017). The efforts of Myanmar indigenous CSOs to work through the aforementioned structural constraints align with arguments that transnational networks have the potential to promote the perspectives of marginalized populations to international spaces (McFarlane 2006). However, realization of a network's potential as a means of empowerment requires a tracing of the discourses within it (Hafner-Burton et al. 2009; McFarlane 2006). As much as a network discourse may provide opportunities for agency, they also pose constraints under structures formed by the distribution of power between actors which directs the flow of ideas and meanings between them (Liljeblad 2023; James 2018; Macpherson 2016; Hook 2007). By controlling communications of ideas and meanings, the power relations in a network impact the outcomes from its discourses (see, for example, Khan & MacEachen 2021; Leifeld 2020; de Almagro 2018; Muller 2015; Della Faille 2011; Mills 2004). The role of power structures in controlling discourse outcomes can encompass global levels of international politics and law (see, for example, Geerlings & Lundberg 2018; Gozzi 2017; Holzscheiter 2014; Kiersey & Stokes 2013). Viewed through notions of discourse, the activities of indigenous peoples in international spaces become illustrations of how actors from subordinate positions can navigate power structures in transnational networks to reach global discourses.

In ascertaining how and when power relations within network operate to constrict or enable subaltern perspectives, it is helpful to clarify additional nuances regarding forms of power that can exist among actors within a network. The literature on international relations offers guidance in describing power as falling into categories of physical power via direct control, economic power through use of material resources, structural power derived from relative positioning in a hierarchy, institutional power provided by rules, moral authority directing normative sensibilities, expert power drawn from specialized knowledge unknown to others, discursive power in the control of language, and network power built on relationships (Moon 2019; Barnett & Duvall 2005). Applied to the scenarios of Myanmar indigenous CSOs, the network discourses for the UPR and UNFCCC exhibited permutations of the above forms of power, with some working to impede Myanmar indigenous activities and others serving to support them.

To begin, with respect to impeding Myanmar indigenous activism, the issues of engagement, access, and outcomes for both the UPR and UNFCCC reflected problems of economic power, structural power, institutional power, expert power, and discursive power. In particular, the state-centric nature of the UPR and UNFCCC meant that in both cases institutional rules created a hierarchy that favored participation by states over non-states, such that institutional power facilitated structural power. With respect to the UPR, UN member states held privileges to pose questions and comments in the Working Group sessions, while non-state actors were relegated to submission of reports to the Working Group, observation of Working Group deliberations, and hosting of side events for state delegates attending the Working Group. The UNFCCC, in comparison, adhered to a hierarchy of three tiers, with state parties having privileges to participate in the Conference of the Parties (CoPs) and other UNFCCC-related bodies; non-state actors admitted to observer status limited to either delivering reports or witnessing UNFCCC body proceedings; and non-state actors without observer status left to engagement with constituency forums or side events. In addition, the processes of the UPR and UNFCCC involved specialized knowledge and skills, with the UPR requiring concepts and principles of international human rights, the UNFCCC tied to concepts and principles of climate change, and both entailing adherence to technical procedures unique to each. The consequence was a merging of expert power, discursive power, and structural power, where the UPR and UNFCCC held practices of discourse calling for particular forms of expertise more likely to be held by states relative to subaltern indigenous peoples. Last, both the UPR and UNFCCC presented costs in terms of attendance, with the UPR incurring travel to Working Group sessions and hosting side events, and the UNFCCC associated with travel to proceedings of multiple disparate bodies and their related side events. Since states were more likely to have the financial resources for such travel, they held an economic power reinforcing their structural privilege over indigenous actors with comparatively less financial means. As a result, the dispositions of the UPR and UNFCCC fostered a bias toward state power in their network discourses.

Those network discourses, however, also provided opportunities that bolstered the power of indigenous voices in mitigating the above forces. Specifically, in the case of the UPR, the networks encompassed intermediaries and social movement alliances that enabled resource-sharing and capacity-building to generate knowledge, skills, and finances to engage UPR processes. While such assistance was not able to alter the privileges for state participation in Working Group sessions, it was sufficient to allow Myanmar indigenous CSOs to conduct side events that allowed direct communications with state delegates to the sessions. In the case of the UNFCCC, the networks included sympathetic actors willing to serve as proxy representatives in addition to delivering capacity-building aid. Without admission to observer status, Myanmar indigenous CSOs were prevented from witnessing the proceedings of UNFCCC bodies, but the support of sympathetic allies meant that they were still able to advance their concerns within side events and constituency bodies. For the network discourses encompassing the UPR and UNFCCC, the primacy of states in the conduct of proceedings was assured, but in both cases, Myanmar indigenous activists were able to find allies that allowed them to find avenues in the network to further their interests.

The resulting image from the experiences of Myanmar indigenous CSOs is that of transnational networks as contested spaces, with the UPR and UNFCCC both reflecting cases where an individual network hosted both features that were disposed against participation by indigenous actors and features that were supportive of the inclusion of indigenous actors. There are several resulting implications for the notions of transnational advocacy networks (TANs) with respect to the aspirations of marginalized voices, the connection between transnational networks and TANs, and the role of advocates within TANs. First, TANs are not always distinct in terms of being isolated but instead may be subsumed within larger transnational networks. As illustrated by the Myanmar indigenous actions with the UPR and UNFCCC, as ambiguous as a network may appear as an aggregate, it may host subsets of actors sympathetic for particular causes. Second, the possibility of TANs embedded within larger networks means that subaltern actors holding marginal status in a given network may still find ways to advance their interests against dominant forces. The potential for subalterns to use a network against hegemonic actors is tied to the identification and selection of sympathetic actors with the will and capacity to render assistance that advances their interests through countervailing power structures in the network. Last, while the allies of Myanmar indigenous CSOs effectively served as TANs within the networks associated with the UPR and UNFCCC, the manner of advocacy was less about speaking on behalf of Myanmar indigenous peoples but instead more about promoting their interests in international venues. In the case of the UPR, the network of sympathetic actors empowered Myanmar indigenous CSOs to make submissions, travel to Working Group sessions, and hold side events to communicate with delegates. In the case of the UNFCCC, the network of allies gave space in observer reports to Myanmar indigenous CSOs, facilitated their travel to UNFCCC venues, and ensured their presence in side events and constituency forums to speak directly with other actors. While they may have operated as proxies, their work did not supplant the voices of Myanmar indigenous CSOs but rather enabled Myanmar indigenous CSOs to speak for themselves. In which case, advocacy was not just representation but also empowerment of otherwise marginalized peoples.

The activities to exercise networks in reaching the UPR and UNFCCC follow patterns of subaltern voices that use networks to engage the hegemony of global forces (Evans 2000), but for Myanmar indigenous CSOs, the goal of agency was not to counter any global-level hegemony connected to the UPR or UNFCCC but rather to direct both global mechanisms to fulfill the purpose of TANs in addressing local issues arising from the domestic hegemony of the Myanmar state. The efforts of Myanmar indigenous CSOs to work through the complexities of the networks associated with the UPR and UNFCCC indicate a commitment to using their respective mechanisms. For both cases, the commitment sustained activism that lasted at least through the course of field research during 2015–2020. Such persistence in the face of structures limiting agency suggests an underlying optimism in terms of a belief that international mechanisms could help to resolve local indigenous issues. In doing so, the experiences of Myanmar indigenous CSOs complement the literature on "bottom-up" studies of indigenous activism vis-à-vis global-level discourses in human rights (Office of the High Commissioner for Human Rights [OHCHR] 2020;

OHCHR 2019; Miranda 2010), climate change (Wani & Ariana 2018; Walbott 2014), and UN (Hasenclever & Narr 2018; Lennox & Short 2016; Anaya 2004a; Anaya 2004b), with the preceding chapters detailing the forms of agency available to further instrumental uses of otherwise state-centric international institutions and rules in service of indigenous peoples' interests.

International law

The notions of transnational networks and discourse fit within the field of International Relations, with issues regarding ideas and meanings such as the substance of human rights and environmental rights for indigenous peoples lying under Constructivist approaches that look to the contestation over norms (see, for example, Klotz & Lynch 2014; Peez 2022; Hafner-Burton et al. 2009). But the UPR and UNFCCC are mechanisms of international law, reflecting institutions and rules for UN agendas on human rights and climate change, respectively. As a result, the analyses of the preceding chapters of this book also connect to the discipline of International Law. In particular, in dealing with the engagement of Myanmar indigenous peoples with the UPR and UNFCCC, they illuminate methods by which indigenous activists can more broadly infiltrate and influence the machinery of international law. Such details offer contributions to several subfields in International Law: Fourth World Approaches to International Law (FWAIL), where the term "Fourth World" refers to the entirety of indigenous peoples within the existing international legal order (see generally Fukurai 2019; Fukurai 2018); Earth Jurisprudence (see generally Schillmoller & Pelizzon 2013; Berry 2011; Cullinan 2011); and Human Rights and Environment. The contributions to each subfield are addressed in the respective subsections below.

FWAIL

FWAIL adopts the term "Fourth World" in reference to global assembly of indigenous peoples in the international order, differentiating their place from the conception of a three-world model of First World states with capitalist economies, Second World states with socialist economies, or Third World states deemed as having underdeveloped economies (Fukurai 2018; Alfred & Corntassel 2005; LaDuke 1983). FWAIL critiques the three-world model as being state-centric, and hence reductionist in its omission of indigenous peoples with distinctive political, legal, economic, and sociocultural systems that existed before—or exists concurrent with—the prevailing state-based Westphalian system of international law (Koot 2020; Watson 2018; Beier 2009; Alfred & Corntassel 2005; Anghie 2004; 2005; 2006; Bruyneel 2007). In addition, FWAIL argues that existing states inherit colonial systems from past European empires that subordinated indigenous peoples under imperial control, such that current states sustain historical patterns of marginalization against indigenous communities lying within their jurisdictions. As a result, in maintaining a primacy of states, the international legal system is continuing a legacy of subjugation, with international institutions and rules serving as a hierarchical structure favoring states and disempowering indigenous peoples (Koot 2020; Watson 2018; Beier 2009; Alfred & Corntassel 2005; Anghie 2004; 2005; 2006; Bruyneel 2007).

There are different approaches within FWAIL toward the relationship between indigenous peoples and international law, with positions that range between "thin" perspectives which support indigenous peoples engaging in the existing international legal system (see, for example, Macklem 2008; Cirkovic 2007; Xanthaki 2000) versus "thick" perspectives that call for an alternative order of international law disconnected from states entirely (Fukurai 2019; Watson 2018; Coulthard 2014; Crossen 2017; Bhatia 2012; Borrows 2006). Between the two extremes is a spectrum of diverse arguments that include acknowledgment of indigenous uses of international law despite its manifestations of colonial power structures (McKeown 2017; Pitts 2017; Anghie 2006; Pahuja 2005), calls to refashion international law in ways for equitable for indigenous peoples (Turner 2006), ideas to reserve spaces for indigenous autonomous governance alongside spaces for participatory indigenous engagement with states (Anaya 2009), or proposals to diversify sources of law in the international system through mutual education of different traditions (Miranda 2010). Others seek to decolonize international law principles (Simpson 2008), explore alliances between indigenous peoples and all marginalized peoples in the international order (Thobani 2008; Gordon 2007), or mobilize resistance against the imperialist aspects of international law (Bhatia 2012; Anghie 2004).

The analyses in the preceding chapters lean more toward the thin perspectives on indigenous peoples and international law, with the experiences of Myanmar indigenous CSOs with the UPR and UNFCCC involving efforts to work within the systems of each. Myanmar indigenous CSOs worked selectively through sympathetic actors within transnational networks to engage the UPR and UNFCCC, but those networks directed their activities in accord with the institutions and rules specific to their respective processes. Myanmar indigenous CSOs may have sought to alter the conduct of the Myanmar state, but they did so by adhering to state-centric procedures in the UPR and UNFCCC. Moreover, Myanmar indigenous CSOs may have been motivated by local issues harming their cultures and lands, but they resorted to knowledge and skills specific to the practices of the UPR and UNFCCC. As a result, as much as the Myanmar indigenous CSOs studied in the preceding chapters displayed agency in their actions vis-à-vis the UPR and UNFCCC, they aligned with FWAIL perspectives that sustained components of an existing state-centric international legal system.

The findings from the preceding chapters, however, contribute to thin approaches in FWAIL by detailing the substance of Myanmar indigenous agency. In particular, the efforts of Myanmar indigenous CSOs vis-à-vis the UPR and UNFCCC serve to identify how indigenous peoples can work within existing international legal mechanisms to advance their interests, even for spaces of international law arguably disposed toward states. Their deployment of multiple strategies in coordinated campaigns to exploit sympathetic subsets of transnational networks offers models for action that add detail to the literature envisioning bottom-up indigenous activism in international human rights (Miranda 2010) and international climate change (NoiseCat 2016). On a more general scale, however, their approaches also help to guide thinking on potential ways to advance indigenous interests within global mechanisms in multiple issue spaces. In doing so, the further the ulterior FWAIL goal of turning attention to the capacities of indigenous peoples vis-à-vis the international legal system, with the ability to bypass the power of states to reach the institutions and rules of international law.

Earth jurisprudence

The contributions to FWAIL approaches also connect to related scholarship on Earth Jurisprudence. Earth Jurisprudence asserts that existing laws, including international law, are predicated on anthropocentric perspectives that render the planet's environment open to exploitation by human civilizations. Earth Jurisprudence seeks to promote systems of law that treat humans as elements within a larger community of life, where the welfare of each member of the community and the community as a whole is determined by the welfare of the planet (Fukurai 2020; Schillmoller & Pelizzon 2013; Cullinan 2011). As a consequence, under Earth Jurisprudence, there is a need to shift from human-centered law to Earth-centered law, since promoting the good of the environment serves to ensure the good of human species (Murray

2015; Murray 2014; Koons 2012; Berry 2011). The arguments of Earth Jurisprudence align with the claims of indigenous peoples with respect to the environment, in that some perspectives of indigeneity define it as involving greater sensitivity to ecosystems and more harmonious coexistence with nature (Clifford 2013; Harkin & Lewis 2007). While not all indigenous peoples identify themselves according to such a criterion, the existence of indigenous cultures that do claim a heritage of sustainable human–nature relationships presents the possibility of functional pre-colonial models of law and governance systems exemplifying Earth Jurisprudence principles (O'Donnell et al. 2020; Humphreys 2017). As a result, Fourth World communities holding to holistic, equitable relationships with the environment present potential guidance for the promotion of Earth Jurisprudence in populations elsewhere. In effect, indigenous peoples and indigenous approaches proffer sources of leadership for Earth Jurisprudence movements (O'Donnell et al. 2020; Knauss 2018; Humphreys 2017).

The work of preceding chapters identifies how indigenous activists can fulfill the expectations for leadership, with the activities of Myanmar indigenous CSOs illuminating avenues for indigenous approaches to the promotion of Earth Jurisprudence concepts in international spaces. The previous chapters demonstrated the linkage of indigenous concerns to issues of human rights and climate change, allowing indigenous interests to enter the deliberations of the UPR and UNFCCC. Thus, to the extent that indigenous concerns encompass Earth Jurisprudence principles, the approaches of Myanmar indigenous CSOs provide a model for other indigenous peoples to elevate Earth Jurisprudence perspectives to the discourses of international human rights and international environmental mechanisms. Similar to the strategies exercised by Myanmar indigenous CSOs, other indigenous activists can identify and ally with sympathetic partners to navigate networks carrying indigenous conceptions of human–nature relationships to spaces of international law, even state-centric ones like the UPR and UNFCCC.

Human rights and environment

The collective analyses of the previous chapters also contribute to the agendas to bridge human rights and environment in international law discourses. At global levels, the work to connect human rights and environment is exemplified by UN efforts that include the specific topical mandate of Special Rapporteur on Human Rights and the Environment (OHCHR 2021i), and the concurrent related mandates of the Special Rapporteur on the Rights of Indigenous Peoples (OHCHR 2021j) and the OHCHR (OHCHR 2021k; OHCHR 2012). Their collective labor has yielded UN guidelines articulating the interdependence of the two fields, with a healthy environment viewed as necessary for the full enjoyment of human rights and the fulfillment of human rights as necessary to ensure promotion of a healthy environment (Human Rights Council [HRC] 2018b; OHCHR 2018). Among the guidelines is Principle 14 in the Framework Principles on Human Rights and Environment, which identifies indigenous peoples as among vulnerable populations at increased risks of damage from environmental harms, violations of human rights, or both (HRC 2018b: Para. 40–41; OHCHR 2018: 20). In particular, Principle 14 states "Indigenous peoples and other traditional communities that rely on their ancestral territories for their material and cultural existence face increasing pressure from Governments … They are usually marginalized from decision-making processes and their rights are often ignored or violated" (HRC 2018b: Para. 41(d); OHCHR 2018: 20). Principle 14 proceeds to call on states to address the risks of vulnerable populations by fashioning laws and policies that recognize their status and enable them to exercise human rights related to the environment (HRC 2018b: Para. 42; OHCHR 2018: 21).

As much as the work of the UN helps to clarify the manifestations of rights between human rights and environments, it would benefit from additional insights in their enforcement. Particularly for indigenous peoples, the expectation of states to follow the aspirational declarations expressed by such instruments as Principle 14 is problematic—as noted by FWAIL critiques, there are continuing patterns of state behavior that marginalize indigenous populations. For an international legal system that favors states, there is a need for accompanying clarity on accountability mechanisms available to indigenous peoples seeking relief against harms arising from state conduct.

The work of the preceding chapters informs such concerns, with the experiences of Myanmar indigenous CSOs illuminating how indigenous peoples can work through components of the international legal system to hold states accountable for harms encompassing human rights and environment. At their core, the studies in the chapters of the present book illustrate an intersection of issues at different levels regarding indigeneity, human rights, and environment. The base scenarios centered around tensions between various peoples and the state over identity, autonomy, and natural resources. To address such tensions, activist groups among those peoples adopted notions of indigenous identity that connected to concepts of human rights and environment. Done in reference to international discourses, the association of the three issue spaces served to frame base tensions in ways amenable to networks related to the international law mechanisms of the UPR and UNFCCC. In effect, global frameworks of indigenous rights, human rights, and environmental rights were linked and overlaid on top of local struggles of Myanmar peoples against the Myanmar state. The efforts to do so were intentional, with the chapters in the present book demonstrating what were essentially intersectional approaches combining indigenous rights, human rights, and environmental discourses to resolve intersectional concerns for the survival of group identities, their respective ways of life, and the related natural resources inherent to both. The work of the organizations studied in the respective chapters points to the depths of their agency in terms of highlighting self-determination in pursuit of self-empowerment to defend self-interests.

The consequence of the above linkages is greater insight regarding the place of indigenous peoples in the discussions bridging human rights and environment, with the experiences of Myanmar indigenous CSOs vis-à-vis the UPR and UNFCCC providing illustrations whose details inform the work to expand understanding of the interconnections between the two topic areas. In doing so, they serve to bridge the mandates of the Special Rapporteur on Human Rights and the Environment, Special Rapporteur on the Rights of Indigenous Peoples, and the OHCHR. As much as the respective agendas of such UN actors have recognized a position for indigenous peoples in the association of human rights and environment, the results of the analyses in the previous chapters illustrate ways for indigenous peoples to accompany that position with action on behalf of their interests amidst the workings of states. They do not constitute a comprehensive sample of options for action, but they do present models of agency offering potential guidance for other indigenous peoples in engaging the global work to integrate human rights and environment together.

On a final note, all of the above comments regarding FWAIL, Earth Jurisprudence, and Human Rights and Environment drew implications from Myanmar indigenous activities *within* the institutions and rules of the UPR and UNFCCC. The insights came from the analyses in the chapters of the book, which identified the challenges posed by the UPR and UNFCCC against indigenous participation and explored the resulting responses of Myanmar indigenous CSOs to overcome those challenges. The consequent implication, however, is for the removal of such challenges altogether. Efforts to do so would serve the larger common goal shared by the above subfields of scholarship of promoting the participation of indigenous peoples. FWAIL's concerns over the subordination of indigenous peoples in international law would be ameliorated by the elevation of indigenous peoples to status comparable to states in international mechanisms; Earth Jurisprudence's goals for the promotion of Earth-centric law would be supported by the increased presence of indigenous voices regarding harmonious human–nature relationships in venues of international law; and the implementation of Human Rights and Environment agendas would be aided by greater indigenous access to accountability mechanisms ensuring state compliance with their principles. In which case, if the interests of international law encompass the aspirations of the above subfields, then there is a subsequent need to also consider ways to remove the obstacles for indigenous participation.

Directions for future research

The attention of the present book was on indigenous agency, with the chapters presenting case studies of Myanmar indigenous activism with respect to global mechanisms of international law. Such activism, however, was specific to the parameters of Myanmar indigenous CSOs engaging the UPR and UNFCCC. As a result, there is a possibility that the insights of the case studies present a limited understanding of more complex phenomena between indigenous peoples and international mechanisms. The goal of greater understanding calls for additional case studies to explore additional areas of indigenous agency, with two directions that could potentially build upon the analyses in the preceding chapters. First, it is possible to study the efforts of other indigenous groups with the UPR and UNFCCC, using each mechanism as a control to allow comparison of various approaches employed by diverse indigenous activists with the same international law venues. Such comparison would help to determine the extent to which institutions and rules dictate the forms of agency of indigenous peoples and hence proscribe their agency or conversely the extent to which different indigenous peoples employ unique approaches and so maintain their agency. Second, it is also worthwhile to focus on a single indigenous group and observe its engagements with multiple international law mechanisms. Doing so would set a control and enable determination as to how the substance of agency can change across different institutions and rules. The context-specific nature of both directions of comparative research poses a potential reach in scale calling for an open project welcoming contributions from a global scholarly community, particularly from researchers with expertise in particular indigenous populations or particular international law mechanisms.

Another direction for future research is to continue the work of the previous chapters with a longitudinal study. A longitudinal perspective would address the changes that have occurred in Myanmar and its indigenous populations as a result of the February 2021 military coup. The coup meant a removal of an elected civilian government and the installation of military rule, with a junta taking all legislative, executive, and judicial power (Poling & Trudes 2021; *The Guardian* 2021d). The return of military control instigated popular revolt, with widespread street protests, a nationwide civil disobedience movement spanning all ministries at all levels of government, and armed conflict in urban and remote areas (*The Guardian* 2021b; ICG 2021; PRIO 2021; OHCHR 2021m). In an attempt to pacify the country, the military, or Tatmadaw, has escalated tactics of suppression that include declaration of martial law; limitations on internet; restriction of protests; arrests and detentions of opponents and their relatives; and violent techniques of terror, torture, and disappearances (Bloomberg 2021; Tran 2021; UN News 2021). Concomitant with such activities has been an intensification of conflict with ethnic armed groups (EAOs) and an acceleration of natural resource extraction to finance Tatmadaw activities (EIA 2021a; EIA 2021b; ICCA Consortium 2021; OHCHR 2021m). The Tatmadaw's actions have received condemnation from the UN for its human rights violations (OHCHR 2021l; OHCHR 2021m; UNSC 2021; *Washington Post* 2021). The UPR session on Myanmar occurred in January 2021 (HRC 2021a), so it did not have comments regarding the coup. But its position as a mechanism under the UN HRC suggests that it would follow the critiques against the Tatmadaw being issued by other offices of the UN. For its part, the UNFCCC CoP 26 convened in October–November 2021 in the wake of the coup, and at the CoP events in Glasgow conference organizers barred the Tatmadaw delegation from participation (RFA 2021).

Myanmar's post-coup conditions are not promising for Myanmar society as a whole. For its indigenous peoples, in particular, they present a state likely to be more inhospitable to claims of indigenous rights, human rights, and environmental rights, especially those referencing international discourses with the potential to challenge the authority of the military regime. As a consequence, while the coup may have escalated the urgency of Myanmar indigenous issues, Myanmar indigenous activists may need to alter their strategies to address the expanded constraints and increased violence of the Tatmadaw. The actions of the Tatmadaw may render the mechanisms of international law more sympathetic to the plight of Myanmar's diverse peoples. As a result, it is possible that Myanmar indigenous peoples may find additional avenues for action beyond the UPR or UNFCCC, with potential opportunities for support via other international mechanisms holding similar mandates related to indigenous rights, human rights, or environmental issues. Pursuit of such opportunities, however, will require increased capacities, further challenging the struggles of Myanmar's indigenous peoples. The exigencies of Myanmar may call for greater engagement with international rights discourses, but to do so will call for greater agency by Myanmar's indigenous peoples in their contest for survival and human dignity.

Bibliography

Aguon, Julia. (2010) On Loving the Maps Our Hands Cannot Hold: Self-Determination of Colonized & Indigenous Peoples in International Law. *UCLA Asian Pacific American Law Journal* 16(1): 47–73.

Alfred, Taiaiake. (2005) *Wasase: Indigenous Pathways of Action & Freedom.* Broadview Press.

Alfred, Taiaiake & Jeff Corntassel. (2005) Being Indigenous: Resurgences Against Contemporary Colonialism. *Government & Opposition* 40(4): 597–614.

Anaya, James. (2004a) *Indigenous Peoples in International Law.* Oxford University Press.

Anaya, James. (2004b) International Human Rights & Indigenous Peoples: The Move Toward the Multicultural State. *Arizona Journal of International & Comparative Law* 21(1): 13–61.

Anaya, James. (2009) *International Human Rights & Indigenous Peoples.* Aspen.

Anaya, James. (2012) *The Role of the UN Special Rapporteur on the Rights of Indigenous Peoples within the United Nations Human Rights System.* University of Arizona. Available at: www.ohchr.org/EN/Issues/IPeoples/IPeoplesFund/Pages/HumanRightsCouncilUniversalPeriodicReview.aspx

Anghie, Antony. (2005) *Imperialism, Sovereignty, & the Making of International Law.* Cambridge University Press.

Anghie, Antony. (2006) The Evolution of International Law: Colonial & Postcolonial Realities. *Third World Quarterly* 27(5): 739–753.

Asia Indigenous Peoples Pact (AIPP). (2012) *AIPP Constitution & By Laws.* Available at: https://aippnet.org/wp-content/uploads/2020/11/AIPP-Constitution-and-By-Laws-ENG.pdf

Asia Indigenous Peoples Pact (AIPP). (2015) *Asia Report on Climate Change.* Available at: www.iipfcc.org/reports

Asia Indigenous Peoples Pact (AIPP). (2017a) *AIPP Chairperson Delivered Asia Indigenous Peoples' Statement in the High Level Opening Session of Indigenous Peoples' Day CoP 23.* Available at: https://aippnet.org/aipp-chairperson-delivered-asia-indigenous-peoples-statement-in-the-high-level-opening-session-of-indigenous-peoples-day-in-the-cop23/

Asia Indigenous Peoples Pact (AIPP). (2017b) *AIPP Side Event @CoP 23*. Available at: www.google.com/url?sa=t&rct=j&q=&esrc=s&source= web&cd=&cad=rja&uact=8&ved=2ahUKEwiekqqRl730AhVWT2wGHSv 9ApAQFnoECAsQAQ&url=https%3A%2F%2Fwww.facebook.com%2Fm edia%2Fset%2F%3Fset%3Da.1543875865702775.1073741830.3489240851 97965%26type%3D3&usg=AOvVaw3l6jc2yhiuCljxt8FM_uV_

Asia Indigenous Peoples Pact (AIPP). (2020) *AIPP-IWGIA Joint Submission: Views from Parties, Indigenous Peoples Organizations, Observers & Other Stakeholders on Existing Politics, Actions, & Communications Including NDCs, NAPs, & Other Relevant Policies & Communications Under the UNFCCC, with Respect to Whether & How They Incorporate Consideration & Engagement of Indigenous Peoples & Local Communities.* Available at: www4.unfccc.int/sites/SubmissionsStaging/Documents/202009012224--- Final_AIPP_IWGIA_Submission_1_September_2020.pdf

Asia Indigenous Peoples Pact (AIPP). (2021) *Asia Indigenous Peoples Pact.* Available at: https://aippnet.org/about-us/

Asia-Pacific Forum (APF). (2015) *Myanmar's NHRI Expands Education and Prison Monitoring Activities.* Available at: www.asiapacificforum.net/news/ myanmars-nhri-expands-education-and-prison-monitoring-activities/

Baird, Ian. (2016) Indigeneity in Asia: An Emerging but Contested Concept. *Asian Ethnicity* 17(4): 501–505.

Baird, Ian. (2020) Thinking about Indigeneity with Respect to Time & Space: Reflections from Southeast Asia. *Space Populations Societies* 2020(1–2). Available at: https://journals.openedition.org/eps/9628

Baird, Ian, Prasit Leepreecha, & Urai Yangcheesutjarit. (2017) Who Should Be Considered "Indigenous"? A Survey of Ethnic Groups in Northern Thailand. *Asian Ethnicity* 18(4): 543–562.

Ball, Jessica & Pauline Janyst. (2008) Enacting Research Ethics in Partnerships with Indigenous Communities in Canada: "Do It in a Good Way." *Journal of Empirical Research on Human Research Ethics: An International Journal* 3(2): 33–51.

Barnard, Alan. (1998) Hunter-Gatherers & Bureaucrats: Reconciling Opposing Worldviews, in Sidsel Saugestad (ed.), *Indigenous Peoples in Modern Nation-States: Proceedings from an International Workshop, University of Tromso, October 13–16, 1997.* 63–76. Faculty of Social Science, University of Tromso.

Barnard, Alan. (2006) Kalahari Revisionism, Vienna, & the "Indigenous Peoples" Debate. *Social Anthropology* 14(1): 1–16.

Barnard, Alan. (2019) *Bushmen: Kalahari Hunter-Gatherers & Their Descendants.* Cambridge University Press.

Barnett, Michael & Raymond Duvall. (2005) Power in International Politics. *International Organization* 59(1): 39–75.

Baviskar, Amita. (2007) Indian Indigeneities: Adivasi Engagements with Hindu Nationalism, in M. de la Cardena & O. Starn (eds.), *Indigenous Experience Today.* 275–304. Berg.

Bayart, Jean-Francois. (1993) *The State in Africa.* Longman.

Beach, Hugh. (2007) "Self-determining the Self: Aspects of Saami Identity Management in Sweden." *Acta Borealis* 24(1): 1–25.

Beier, J. Marshall. (2007) Inter-National Affairs: Indigeneity, Globality, & the Canadian State. *Canadian Foreign Policy Journal* 13(3): 121–131.

Beier, J. Marshall. (2009) *Indigenous Diplomacies*. Palgrave Macmillan.

Belfer, Ella, James Ford, & Michelle Maillat. (2017) Representation of Indigenous Peoples in Climate Change Reporting. *Climate Change* 145(2017): 57–70.

Belfer, Ella, James Ford, Michelle Maillat, Malcolm Araos, & Melanie Flynn. (2019) Pursuing an Indigenous Platform: Exploring Opportunities & Constraints for Indigenous Participation in the UNFCCC. *Global Environmental Politics* 19(1): 12–33.

Bello-Bravo, Julia. (2019) When Is Indigeneity: Closing a Legal & Sociocultural Gap in a Contested Domestic/International Term. *AlterNative* 15(2): 111–120.

Berger, Peter. (2014) Dimensions of Indigeneity in Highland Odisha, India. *Asian Ethnology* 73(1–2): 19–37.

Berry, Thomas. (2011) Rights of the Earth: We Need a New Legal Framework Which Recognizes the Rights of All Living Beings, in Peter Burdon (ed.), *Exploring Wild Law: The Philosophy of Earth Jurisprudence*. 227–229. Wakefield.

Bettiza, Gregorio & Filippo Dionigi. (2015) How Do Religious Norms Diffuse? Institutional Translation and International Change in a Post-Secular World Society. *European Journal of International Relations* 21(3): 621–646.

Bhatia, Amar. (2012) The South of the North: Building on Critical Approaches to International Law with Lessons from the Fourth World. *Oregon Review of International Law* 14(2012): 131–175.

Blackburn, Carole. (2009) Differentiating Indigenous Citizenship: Seeking Multiplicity in Rights, Identity, & Sovereignty in Canada. *American Ethnologist* 36(1): 66–78.

Bloomberg. (2021) *Myanmar Deploys Martial Law in Cities as Youths Stare Down Army*. Bloomberg, 8 February 2021. Available at: www.bloomberg.com/news/articles/2021-02-08/myanmar-youth-stare-down-army-with-history-of-killing-protesters

Boer, Ben (ed.). (2015) *Environmental Law Dimensions of Human Rights*. Oxford University Press.

Borrows, John. (2006) *Justice Within: Indigenous Legal Traditions*. Law Commission of Canada. Available at: https://publications.gc.ca/site/eng/9.667883/publication.html?wbdisable=true

Bourke, Brian. (2014) Positionality: Reflecting on the Research Process. *The Qualitative Report* 19(33): 1–9.

Boyle, Alan. (2018) Climate Change, the Paris Agreement, & Human Rights. *International & Comparative Law Quarterly* 67(2018): 759–777.

Brewer II, Joseph & Elizabeth Ann Kronk Warner. (2015) Protecting Indigenous Knowledge in the Age of Climate Change. *Georgetown International Environmental Law Review* 27(4): 585–628.

Brightman, Marc. (2008) Strategic Ethnicity on the Global Stage: Identity & Property in the Global Indigenous Peoples' Movement, from the Central

Guianas to the United Nations. *Swiss Society of the Americas Bulletin* 70(2008): 21–29.

Brown, James & Patricia Sant (eds.). (1999) *Indigeneity: Construction & Re/presentation*. Nova Science Publishers.

Bruyneel, Kevin. (2007) *The Third Space of Sovereignty: The Postcolonial Politics of U.S.-Indigenous Relations*. University of Minnesota Press.

Brysk, Allison. (2000) *From Tribal Village to Global Village: Indian Rights and International Rights in Latin America*. Stanford University Press.

Bureau des Avocats Internationaux. (2011) *Universal Periodic Review: Environmental Justice Report*. Institute for Justice & Democracy in Haiti. Available at: www.ijdh.org/2011/03/topics/housing/universal-periodic-review-environmental-justice-report-association-haitenne-de-droit-de-lenvironnement-environmental-justice-initiative-in-haiti-national-lawyers-guild-environmental-justice-comm/

Burger, Julian. (1987) *Report from the Frontier: The State of the World's Indigenous Peoples*. Zed Books.

Burma–Myanmar Universal Periodic Review Forum (Burma–Myanmar UPR Forum). (2015). *2nd Cycle Universal Periodic Review Myanmar UPR 2015*. Available at: www.upr-info.org/en/news/myanmar-kicking-off-the-upr-follow-up-phase-with-the-burmamyanmar-upr-forum

Cabre, Miquel Munoz. (2011) Issue-Linkages to Climate Change Measured Through NGO Participation in the UNFCCC. *Global Environmental Politics* 11(3): 10–22.

Callahan, Mary. (2003) *Making Enemies: War & State-Building in Burma*. Cornell University Press.

Callahan, Mary. (2012) The Opening in Burma: The Generals Loosen Their Grip. *The Journal of Democracy* 23(2012): 20–131.

Cambou, Dorothee. (2019) The UNDRIP & the Legal Significance of the Right of Indigenous Peoples to Self-Determination: A Human Rights Approach with a Multidimensional Perspective. *The International Journal of Human Rights* 23(1–2): 34–50.

Canessa, Andrew. (2018) Indigenous Conflict in Bolivia Explored Through an African Lens: Towards a Comparative Analysis of Indigeneity. *Comparative Studies in Society & History* 60(2): 308–337.

Canning, Patrick. (2018) I Could Turn You to Stone: Indigenous Blockades in an Age of Climate Change. *International Indigenous Policy Journal* 9(3): 1–32. Available at: https://ir.lib.uwo.ca/iipj/vol9/iss3/7/

Carpenter, R. Charli. (2007) Setting the Advocacy Agenda: Theorizing Issue Emergence and Nonemergence in Transnational Advocacy Networks. *International Studies Quarterly* 51: 99–120.

Castellino, Joshua. (2010) The Protection of Minorities & Indigenous Peoples in International Law: A Comparative Temporal Analysis. *International Journal on Minority & Group Rights* 17(2010): 393–422.

Castleden, Heather, Vanessa Morgan, & Christopher Lamb. (2012) "I Spent the First Year Drinking Tea": Exploring Canadian University Researchers' Perspectives on Community-Based Participatory Research Involving Indigenous Peoples. *The Canadian Geographer* 56(2): 160–179.

Center for International Forestry Research (CIFOR). (2017) *CIFOR @CoP23*. Available at: www2.cifor.org/cifor-at-cop-23/

Center for International Forestry Research (CIFOR). (2021) *Partners*. Available at: www.cifor.org/our-work/partners/

Chalk, Peter. (2013) *On the Path of Change: Political, Economic and Social Challenges for Myanmar*. Australian Strategic Policy Institute. Available at: www.aspi.org.au/publications/on-the-path-of-change-political,-economic-and-social-challenges-for-myanmar/SR62_Myanmar.pdf

Channel News Asia. (2015a) *Myanmar to "Wait and See" on Constitutional Change: Army Chief*. January 28, 2015. Available at: www.channelnewsasia. com/news/asiapacific/myanmar-to-wait-and-see/1612338.html

Channel News Asia. (2015b) *Myanmar's Military Says Will Not Unilaterally Stage a Coup*. January 21, 2015. Available at: www.channelnewsasia.com/ news/asiapacific/myanmar-s-military-says/1606338.html

Channel News Asia. (2015c) *Myanmar Not Ready for Reduced Military Role in Parliament: Army Chief*. January 20, 2015. Available at: www.channelnewsasia. com/news/asiapacific/myanmar-not-ready-for/1603394.html

Charters, Claire. (2010) A Self-determination Approach to Justifying Indigenous Peoples' Participation in International Law & Policy Making. *International Journal on Minority & Group Rights* 17(2010): 215–240.

Chau, Thompson. (2019) Tanintharyi Landholders Sued Under New Law, March 11, 2019. *Myanmar Times*. Available at: www.mmtimes.com/news/ tanintharyi-landholders-sued-under-new-law.html

Cheesman, Nick. (2017) How in Myanmar "National Races" Came to Surpass Citizenship & Exclude Rohingya. *Journal of Contemporary Asia* 47(3): 463.

Cheesman, Nick, Monique Skidmore, & Trevor Wilson (eds.). (2012) *Myanmar's Transition: Openings, Obstacles, and Opportunities*. ISEAS Publishing.

Chen, Cher Weixia. (2017) Indigenous Rights in International Law, in Renee Marlin-Bennett (ed.), *Oxford Research Encyclopedia of International Studies*. Oxford University Press.

Chilisa, Bagele. (2020) *Indigenous Research Methodologies*. Sage.

Chiu, Kuei-fen. (2013) Cosmopolitanism & Indigenism: The Uses of Cultural Authenticity in an Age of Flows. *New Literary History* 44(2013): 159–178.

Christie, Gordon. (2011) Indigeneity & Sovereignty in Canada's Far North: The Arctic & Inuit Sovereignty. *The South Atlantic Quarterly* 110(2): 329–346.

Ciplet, David. (2014) Contesting Climate Injustice: Transnational Advocacy Network Struggles for Rights in UN Climate Politics. *Global Environmental Politics* 14(4): 75–96.

Cirkovic, Elena. (2007) Theoretical Approaches to International Indigenous Rights: Self-Determination & Indigenous Peoples in International Law. *American Indian Law Review* 31(2007): 375–399.

Claeys, Priscilla. (2018) The Rise of New Rights for Peasants: From Resilience on NGO Intermediaries to Direct Representation. *Transnational Legal Theory* 9(3–4): 386–399.

Clifford, James. (1997) *Travel & Translation in the Late Twentieth Century*. Harvard University Press.

Clifford, James. (2013) *Returns: Becoming Indigenous in the Twenty-First Century*. Harvard University Press.

Coalition of Indigenous Peoples in Myanmar/Burma (CIPM). (2015) *JS7 Joint Submission to the UN Universal Periodic Review of Myanmar, March 2015 for the 23rd Session of the UPR Working Group of the Human Rights Council, November 2015*. Burma Library. Available at: www.burmalibrary. org/docs21/NEED-Coalition_of_IPs_in_Myanmar-2015-03-Submission_ to_UPR-en-red.pdf

Coalition of Indigenous Peoples in Myanmar/Burma (CIPM). (2020) *JS11 Joint Submission to the UN Universal Periodic Review of Myanmar, July 2020 for the 37th Session of the UPR Working Group of the Human Rights Council, January/February 2021*. Office of the High Commissioner for Human Rights. Available at: https://uprdoc.ohchr.org/uprweb/downloadfile.aspx?filename= 8278&file=EnglishTranslation

Coates, Ken. (2004) *A Global History of Indigenous Peoples*. Palgrave Macmillan.

Cobo, Jose R. Martinez. (1982) *Study of the Problem of Discrimination against Indigenous Populations, Final Report (Supplementary Part) Submitted By the Special Rapporteur Mr. Jose R. Martinez Cobo, E/CN.4/Sub.2/1982/2/Add.6*. United Nations Economic & Social Council. Available at: www.un.org/esa/ socdev/unpfii/documents/MCS_v_en.pdf

Comberti, Claudia, et al. (2019) Adaptation & Resilience at the Margins: Addressing Indigenous Peoples' Marginalization at International Climate Negotiations. *Environment: Science & Policy for Sustainable Development* 61(2): 14–30.

Committee on the Elimination of All Forms of Racial Discrimination (CERD). (1997) *General Recommendation 23 on the Rights of Indigenous Peoples A/ 52/18 Annex V*. Available at: https://tbinternet.ohchr.org/_layouts/15/ treatybodyexternal/TBSearch.aspx?Lang=en&TreatyID=6&DocTypeID= 11&ctl00_PlaceHolderMain_radResultsGridChangePage=2

Conklin, Beth. (2002) Shamans Versus Pirates in the Amazonian Treasure Chest. *American Anthropologist* 104(4): 1050–1061.

Convention on Biological Diversity (CBD). (1992) Available at: www.cbd.int/ convention/text/

Cooke, Fadzilah Majid & Sofia Johari. (2019) Positioning of Murut & Bajau Identities in State Forest Reserves & Marine Parks in Sabah, East Malaysia. *Journal of Southeast Asian Studies* 50(1): 129–149.

Corntassel, Jeff & Tomas Primeau. (2006) Indigenous "Sovereignty" & International Law: Revised Strategies for Pursuing "Self-Determination." *Hawaiian Journal of Law & Politics* 2(2006): 52–72.

Coulthard, Glen. (2014) *Red Skin, White Masks: Rejecting the Colonial Politics of Recognition*. University of Minnesota Press.

Crossen, Jonathan. (2017) Another Wave of Anti-Colonialism: The Origins of Indigenous Internationalism. *Canadian Journal of History* 52(3): 533–559.

Crouch, Melissa & Tim Lindsey (eds.). (2014) *Law, Society, and Transition in Myanmar*. Hart Publishing.

Cullinan, Cormac. (2011) A History of Wild Law, in Peter Burdon (ed.), *Exploring Wild Law: The Philosophy of Earth Jurisprudence*. 12–23. Wakefield.

Cultural Survival. (2015) *Universal Periodic Review: A Potent Process for the Realization of Human Rights in Indigenous Homelands*. Cultural Survival. Available at: www.culturalsurvival.org/publications/cultural-survival-quarterly/universal-periodic-review-potent-process-realization-human

Cuso International (Cuso). (2019) *Groups, Southeast Asian Indigenous Women Leaders to CoP 25 Delegates: Stronger Climate Adaptation Support Now!* Available at: https://cusointernational.org/news/groups-southeast-asian-indigenous-women-leaders-to-cop-25-delegates-stronger-climate-adaptation-support-now/

Cuso International (Cuso). (2021) *Finances & Accountability*. Available at: https://cusointernational.org/impact/finances-and-accountability/

Dahl, Jens. (2009) *IWGIA: A History*. International Work Group on Indigenous Affairs. Available at: www.iwgia.org/en/about.html

Dahl, Jens. (2012) *The Indigenous Space and Marginalized Peoples in the United Nations*. Palgrave Macmillan.

David, Roman & Ian Holliday. (2019) *Liberalism & Democracy in Myanmar*. Oxford University Press.

Davies, Mathew. (2010) Rhetorical Inaction? Compliance and the Human Rights Council of the United Nations. *Alternatives* 35: 449–468.

Davis, Shelton. (2010) Indigenous Peoples & Climate Change. *International Indigenous Policy Journal* 1(1): 1–17. Available at: https://ir.lib.uwo.ca/iipj/vol1/iss1/2/

De Almagro, Maria Martin. (2018) Lost Boomerangs, the Rebound Effect, & Transnational Advocacy Networks: A Discursive Approach to Norm Diffusion. *Review of International Studies* 44(4): 672–693.

De la Cadena, Marisol & Orin Starn. (2007) *Indigenous Experience Today*. Routledge.

Della Faille, Dimitri. (2011) Discourse Analysis in International Development Studies: Mapping Some Contemporary Contributions. *Journal of Multicultural Discourses* 6(3): 215–235.

Della Porta, Donna & Sidney Tarrow (eds.). (2004) *Transnational Protest & Global Activism*. Rowman & Littlefield.

Della Porta, Donatella, Massimiliano Andretta, Lorenza Mosca, & Herbert Reiter. (2006) *Globalization from Below*. University of Minnesota Press.

Diamond, Larry. (2012) The Need for a Political Pact. *Journal of Democracy* 23(4): 138–149.

Dittmer, Lowell (ed.). (2010) *Burma or Myanmar? The Struggle for National Identity*. World Scientific Publishing Company.

DOCIP: Centre de Documentation, de Recherche, et D'Information des Peoples Autochtones (DOCIP). (2021). *Saw Mae Plet Htoo, Karen National Union, Working Group on Indigenous Populations*. Available at: https://cendoc.docip.org/cgi-bin/library.cgi?e=d-00100-00---off-0cendocdo--00-2---0-10-0---0---0direct-10----4-------0-1l--10-fr-50---20-home-Ati+QUIGUA--00-3-21-00-10--4--0--0-0-01-10-0utfZz-8-00&a=d&c=cendocdo&cl=CL3.3.4.158

Dombrowski, Kirk. (2002) The Praxis of Indigenism & Alaska Native Timber Politics. *American Anthropologist* 104(4): 1062–1073.

Doolittle, Amity. (2010) The Politics of Indigeneity: Indigenous Strategies for Inclusion in Climate Change Negotiations. *Conservation & Society* 8(4): 286–291.

Dorough, Dalee Sambo. (2016) The Ongoing Indigenous Political Enterprise: What's Law Got to Do with It. *Journal of Law, Property, & Society* 2(2016): i-93.

Dunbar-Ortiz, Roxanne, Dalee Sambo Dorough, Gudmundr Alfredsson, Lee Swepston, & Peter Willie. (2015) *Indigenous Peoples' Rights in International Law: Emergence & Application*. Galdu & IWGIA. Available at: www.iwgia. org/images/publications/0709_INDIGENOUS_PEOPLES_RIGHTS_ 2.pdf

Dunford, Michael. (2019) Indigeneity, Ethnopolitics, & Taingyinthar: Myanmar & the Global Indigenous Peoples' Movement. *Journal of Southeast Asian Studies* 50(1): 51–67.

Duyck, Sebastien, Erika Lennon, Wolfgang Obergassel, & Annalisa Savaresi. (2018) Human Rights and the Paris Agreement's Implementation Guidelines: Opportunities to Develop a Rights-Based Approach. *Carbon & Climate Law Review* 12(3): 191–202.

Egreteau, Renaud. (2014) Legislators in Myanmar's First "Post-Junta" National Parliament (2010–2015): A Sociological Analysis. *Journal of Southeast Asian Affairs* 33(2): 91–124.

Eichler, Jessika. (2018) Indigenous Intermediaries in Prior Consultation Processes: Bridge Builders or Silenced Voices? *Journal of Latin American & Caribbean Anthropology* 23(3): 560–578.

Eide, Asbjorn. (2009) The Indigenous Peoples, the Working Group on Indigenous Populations & the Adoption of the UN Declaration of the Rights of Indigenous Peoples, in Claire Charters & Rodolfo Stavenhagen (eds.), *Making the Declaration Work: The United Nations Declaration on the Rights of Indigenous Peoples*. 32–47. IWGIA. Available at: www.iwgia.org/ images/publications/making_the_declaration_work.pdf

Einzenberger, Rainer. (2016) Contested Frontiers: Indigenous Mobilization & Control Over Land & Natural Resources in Myanmar's Upland Areas. *Austrian Journal of South-East Asian Studies* 9(1): 163–172.

Engineering & Technology. (2021) *Myanmar's Military Coup Linked to Illegal Deforestation*. Available at: https://eandt.theiet.org/content/articles/2021/04/ myanmar-s-military-coup-linked-to-illegal-deforestation/

Englehart, Neil. (2012) Two Cheers for Burma's Rigged Election. *Asian Survey* 52(2012): 666–686.

Environmental Investigation Agency (EIA). (2021a) *Myanmar's Tainted Timber & the Military Coup*. Available at: https://eia-international.org/forests/ myanmars-tainted-timber-and-the-military-coup/

Environmental Investigation Agency (EIA). (2021b) *Myanmar Junta Looks to Line Its Pockets & Fund the Coup with Massive Auction of Illegal Timber*. Available at: https://eia-international.org/news/myanmar-junta-looks-to-line-its-pockets-and-fund-the-coup-with-massive-auction-of-illegal-timber/

Erni, Christian. (ed.) (2008) *The Concept of Indigenous Peoples in Asia: A Resource Book, IWGIA Document No. 123. Indigenous Work Group for*

Indigenous Affairs. Available at: www.iwgia.org/images/publications/ Concept_of_Indigenous_Peoples_in_Asia_-_Digital.pdf

Escarcega, Sylvia. (2010) Authenticating Strategic Essentialisms: The Politics of Indigenousness at the United Nations. *Cultural Dynamics* 22(1): 3–28.

Escarcega, Sylvia. (2012) The Global Indigenous Movement and Paradigm Wars, in Jeffrey Juris & Alex Khasnabish (eds.), *Insurgent Encounters*. 129–150. Duke University Press.

Escobar, Arturo. (2008) *Territories of Difference: Place, Movements, Life, Redes*. Duke University Press.

Etchart, Linda. (2017) The Role of Indigenous Peoples in Combating Climate Change. *Palgrave Communications* 3(2017). Available at: https://doi.org/ 10.1057/palcomms.2017.85

Ethnic Rights Protection Law (ERPL). (2015) *Myanmar Ethnic Rights Protection Law 2015*. Available at: www.mlis.gov.mm/mLsView. do;jsessionid=8FB0DEC085CB41D632D97FB902665567?lawordSn= 9701

Evans, Peter. (2000) Fighting Marginalization with Transnational Networks: Counter-Hegemonic Globalization. *Contemporary Sociology* 29(1): 230–241.

Expert Mechanism on the Rights of Indigenous Peoples (EMRIP). (2021) *Expert Mechanism on the Rights of Indigenous Peoples*. Office of the High Commissioner for Human Rights (OHCHR). Available at: www.ohchr.org/ EN/Issues/IPeoples/EMRIP/Pages/EMRIPIndex.aspx

Farr, Jason. (2005) Point: The Westphalia Legacy & the Modern Nation-State. *International Social Science Review* 80(3/4): 156–159.

Farrelly, Nicholas. (2014) Cooperation, Contestation, Conflict: Ethnic Political Interests in Myanmar Today. *South East Asia Research* 22(2): 251–266.

Ferguson, Jane. (2015) Who's Counting? Ethnicity, Belonging, & the National Census in Burma/Myanmar. *Bijdragen Tot de Taal, Land-en Volkenkunde/ Journal of the Humanities & Social Sciences of Southeast Asia* 171(2015): 1–28.

Fernandez-Llamazares, Alvaro, et al. (2015) Links Between Media Communication & Local Perceptions of Climate Change in an Indigenous Society. *Climatic Change* 131(2015): 307–320.

FIDH. (2015) *Burma: UPR Commitments Remain Largely Unaddressed*. Available at: www.fidh.org/International-Federation-for-Human-Rights/ asia/burma/burma-upr-commitments-remain-largely-unaddressed

Fink, Christina. (2014) How Real Are Myanmar's Reforms? *Current History* 2014: 224–229.

Finnemore, Margaret & Kathryn Sikkink. (1998) International Norm Dynamics and Political Change. *International Organization* 52: 887–917.

Fodella, Alessandro. (2006) International Law & the Diversity of Indigenous Peoples. *Vermont Law Review* 30(3): 565–594.

Ford, James, et al. (2016) Adaptation & Indigenous Peoples in the United Nations Framework Convention on Climate Change. *Climatic Change* 139(2016): 429–443.

Forte, Maximilian (ed.) (2010) *Indigenous Cosmopolitanisms: Transnational and Transcultural Indigeneity in the Twenty-First Century*. Peter Lang International Academic Publishers.

French, Jan Hoffman. (2011) The Power of Definition: Brazil's Contribution to Universal Concepts of Indigeneity. *Indiana Journal of Global Legal Studies* 18(1): 241–261.

Fukurai, Hiroshi. (2018) Fourth World Approaches to International Law (FWAIL) & Asia's Indigenous Struggles & Quests for Recognition Under International Law. *Asian Journal of Law & Society* 5(2018): 221–231.

Fukurai, Hiroshi. (2019) Original Nation Approaches to "Inter-National" Law (ONAIL): Decoupling of the Nation & the State & the Search for New Legal Orders. *Indiana Journal of Global Legal Studies* 26(1): 199–262.

Fukurai, Hiroshi. (2020) The Decoupling of the Nation & the State: Constitutionalizing Transnational Nationhood, Cross-Border Connectivity, Diaspora, & "National" Identity-Affiliation in Asia & Beyond. *Asian Journal of Law & Society* 7(2020): 1–4.

Gagne, Natacha. (2012) The Study of Colonial Situations: The Emergence of a New General Approach? *Reviews in Anthropology* 41(2): 109–135.

Gagne, Natacha. (2015) Brave New Words: The Complexities & Possibilities of an "Indigenous" Identity in French Polynesia & New Caledonia. *The Contemporary Pacific* 27(2): 371–402.

Ganesan, Narayanan. (2013) Interpreting Recent Developments in Myanmar as an Attempt to Establish Political Legitimacy. *Asian Journal of Peacebuilding* 1(2013): 253–274.

Garcia, Beatriz & Lucas Lixinski. (2020) Beyond Culture: Reimagining the Adjudication of Indigenous Peoples' Rights in International Law. *Intercultural Human Rights Law Review* 15(2020): 127–170.

Geerlings, Lennie & Anita Lundberg. (2018) Global Discourses & Power/ Knowledge: Theoretical Reflections on Futures of Higher Education During the Rise of Asia. *Asia Pacific Journal of Education* 38(2): 229–240.

Gerharz, Eva. (2014) Recognising Indigenous People, the Bangladeshi Way: The United Nations Declaration for Indigenous Peoples' Rights, Transnational Activism, & the Constitutional Amendment Affair of 2011. *Indigenous Policy Journal* 24(4): 64–79.

Gerharz, Eva, Nasir Uddin, & Pradeep Chakkarath. (2018) *Indigeneity on the Move: Varying Manifestations of a Contested Concept.* Berghahn.

Gerlach, Allen. (2003) *Indians, Oil, & Politics: A Recent History of Ecuador.* Scholarly Resources Incorporated.

Gerrard, Emily. (2008) Climate Change & Human Rights: Issues & Opportunities for Indigenous Peoples. *University of New South Wales Law Journal* 31(3): 941–952.

Golan, Daphna & Zvika Orr. (2012) Translating Human Rights of the "Enemy": The Case of Israeli NGOs Defending Palestinian Rights. *Law & Society Review* 46(4): 781–814.

Gombay, Nicole & Marcela Palomino-Schalscha (eds.). (2018) *Indigenous Places & Colonial Spaces: Forging Indigenous Places in Intertwined Worlds.* Routledge.

Gomes, Alberto. (2013) Anthropology & the Politics of Indigeneity. *Anthropological Forum* 23(1): 5–15.

Goodale, Mark. (2006) Reclaiming Modernity: Indigenous Cosmopolitanism & the Coming of the Second Revolution in Bolivia. *American Ethnologist* 33(4): 634–649.

Godden, Lee & Maureen Tehan. (2016) REDD+: Climate Justice & Indigenous & Local Community Rights in an Era of Climate Disruption. *Journal of Energy & Natural Resources Law* 34(1): 95–108.

Goodman, Nicole, Karen Bird, & Chelsea Gabel. (2017) Towards a More Collaborative Political Science: A Partnership Approach. *Canadian Journal of Political Science* 50(1): 201–218.

Gordon, Seth. (2007) Indigenous Rights in Modern International Law from a Critical Third World Perspective. *American Indian Law Review* 32(2): 401–424.

Gozzi, Gustavo. (2017) The "Discourse" of International Law & Humanitarian Intervention. *Ratio Juris* 30(2): 186–204.

Grear, Anna & Louis Kotze. (2015) *Research Handbook on Human Rights and the Environment*. Edward Elgar Publishing.

Green, Joyce. (2009) The Complexity of Indigenous Identity Formation & Politics in Canada: Self-Determination & Decolonisation. *International Journal of Critical Indigenous Studies* 2(2): 36–46.

Greene, Shane. (2006) Getting Over the Andes: The Geo-Eco-Politics of Indigenous Movements of Indigenous Movements in Peru's Twenty-First Century Inca Empire. *Journal of Latin American Studies* 38(2006): 327–354.

Gregg, Benjamin. (2019) Indigeneity as Social Construct & Political Tool. *Human Rights Quarterly* 41(4): 823–848.

Griggs, Richard. (1992) *The Meaning of "Nation" and "State" in the Fourth World*. Center for World Indigenous Studies.

Guenther, Mathias. (2006) The Concept of Indigeneity. *Social Anthropology* 14(1): 17–32.

Guidry, J.A., Michael Kennedy, & Mayer Zald. (2000) *Globalizations and Social Movements*. University of Michigan Press.

Hafner-Burton, Emilie, Miles Kahler, & Alexander Montgomery. (2009) Network Analysis for International Relations. *International Organization* 63(3): 559–592.

Hall, Thomas & James Fenelon. (2009) *Indigenous Peoples & Globalization*. Paradigm Publishers.

Harkin, Michael & David Lewis (eds.). (2007) *Native Americans & the Environment*. University of Nebraska Press.

Harry, Debra. (2011) Biocolonialism & Indigenous Knowledge in United Nations Discourse. *Griffith Law Review* 20(3): 702–728.

Hart, Michael, Silvia Straka, & Gladys Rowe. (2017) Working Across Contexts: Practical Considerations of Doing Indigenist/Anto-Colonial Research. *Qualitative Inquiry* 23(5): 332–342.

Hasenclever, Andreas & Henrike Narr. (2018) The Dark Side of the Affectedness-Paradigm: Lessons from the Indigenous Peoples' Movement at the United Nations. *Third World Thematics* 3(5–6): 684–702.

Havemann, Paul. (2009) Ignoring the Mercury in the Climate Change Barometer: Denying Indigenous Peoples' Rights. *Australian Indigenous Law Review* 13(1): 2–26.

Hays, Jennifer & Megan Biesele. (2011) Indigenous Rights in Southern Africa: International Mechanisms & Local Contexts. *The International Journal of Human Rights* 15(1): 1–10.

Heinamaki, Leena. (2009) Rethinking the Status of Indigenous Peoples in International Environmental Decision-Making: Pondering the Role of Arctic Indigenous Peoples & the Challenge of Climate Change, in T. Koivurova, E. Keskitalo, & N. Bankes (eds.), *Climate Governance in the Arctic.* 250–279. Springer.

Held, David & Antony McGrew. (2002) *Globalization/Anti-Globalization.* Polity Press.

Henderson, James. (2008) *Indigenous Diplomacy & the Rights of Peoples: Achieving UN Recognition.* Purich Publishing Limited.

Henriksen, John. (2001) "Implementation of the Right of Self-Determination of Indigenous Peoples." *Indigenous Affairs* 3(1): 6–21.

Hernandez-Avila, Ines. (2003) The Power of Native Languages & the Performance of Indigenous Autonomy: The Case of Mexico, in Richard Grounds, George Tinker, & David Wilkins (eds.), *Native Voices: American Indian Identity & Resistance.* University of Kansas Press.

Higgins, Noelle. (2014) Advancing the Rights of Minorities & Indigenous Peoples: Getting UN Attention via the Universal Periodic Review. *Netherlands Quarterly of Human Rights* 32(4): 379–407.

Higgins, Noelle. (2019) Creating a Space for Indigenous Rights: The Universal Periodic Review as a Mechanism Promoting the Rights of Indigenous Peoples. *International Journal of Human Rights* 23(1–2): 125–148.

Hlaing, Kyaw Yin. (2012) Understanding Recent Political Changes in Myanmar. *Contemporary Southeast Asia* 34(2012): 197–216.

Hochstetler, Kathryn & Margaret Keck. (2007) *Greening Brazil: Environmental Activism in State and Society.* Duke University Press.

Hodgson, Dorothy. (2002a) Introduction: Comparative Perspectives on the Indigenous Rights Movement in Africa & the Americas. *American Anthropologist* 104(4): 1037–1049.

Hodgson, Dorothy. (2002b) Precarious Alliances: The Cultural Politics & Structural Predicaments of the Indigenous Rights Movement in Tanzania. *American Anthropologist* 104(4): 1086–1097.

Hodgson, Dorothy. (2009) Becoming Indigenous in Africa. *African Studies Review* 52(3): 1–32.

Hodgson, Dorothy. (2011) *Being Maasai, Becoming Indigenous: Postcolonial Politics in a Neoliberal World.* Indiana University Press.

Holm, Tom, Diane Pearson, & Ben Chavis. (2003) Peoplehood: A Model for American Indian Sovereignty in Education. *Wicazo Sa Review* 18(2003): 7–24.

Holzscheiter, Anna. (2014) Between Communicative Interaction & Structures of Signification: Discourse Theory & Analysis in International Relations. *International Studies Perspectives* 15(2): 142–162.

Hook, Derek (2007) *Foucault, Psychology, & the Analytics of Power.* Palgrave Macmillan.

Huang, Hsinya. (2014) Indigenous Taiwan as Location of Native American & Indigenous Studies. *CLCWeb: Comparative Literature & Culture* 16(4). Available at: https://docs.lib.purdue.edu/clcweb/vol16/iss4/2/

Huelshoff, Michael & Christina Kiel. (2012) Swan Song: Transnational Advocacy Networks and Environmental Policy in Chile—The Case of the Cisnes de Cuello Negro. *Interest Groups & Advocacy* 1: 260–278.

Human Rights Council (HRC). (2009) *Tenth Session, Resolution 10/4. Human Rights & Climate Change.* Available at: https://ap.ohchr.org/documents/E/HRC/resolutions/A_HRC_RES_10_4.pdf

Human Rights Council (HRC). (2013) *Mapping Human Rights Obligations Relating to the Enjoyment of a Safe, Clean, Healthy and Sustainable Environment: Individual Report on the UN General Assembly and the Human Rights Council, Including the Universal Periodic Review Process, Report No. 6.* United Nations. Available at: www.ohchr.org/Documents/Issues/Environment/MappingReport/6.HRC-UPR-25-Feb.docx

Human Rights Council (HRC). (2015) *Summary Prepared By the Office of the United Nations High Commissioner for Human Rights in Accordance with Paragraph 15(c) of the Annex to the Human Rights Council Resolution 5/1 and Paragraph 5 of the Annex to Council Resolution 16/21,* A/HRC/WG.6/23/MMR/3. United Nations General Assembly. Available at: http://daccess-ods.un.org/access.nsf/Get?Open&DS=A/HRC/WG.6/23/MMR/3&Lang=E

Human Rights Council (HRC). (2016) *Report of the Special Rapporteur on the Issue of Human Rights Obligations Relating to the Enjoyment of a Safe, Clean, Healthy, and Sustainable Environment, UN Doc A/HRC/31/52.* Available at: https://undocs.org/A/HRC/31/52

Human Rights Council (HRC). (2018a) *Framework Principles on Human Rights & the Environment A/HRC/37/59.* Office of the High Commissioner for Human Rights. Available at: www.ohchr.org/EN/Issues/Environment/SREnvironment/Pages/FrameworkPrinciplesReport.aspx

Human Rights Council (HRC). (2018b) *Report of the Special Rapporteur on the Issue of Human Rights Obligations Relating to the Enjoyment of a Safe, Clean, Healthy, & Sustainable Environment, A/HRC/37/59.* Available at: https://undocs.org/A/HRC/37/59

Human Rights Council (HRC). (2021a) *Universal Periodic Review——Myanmar.* Available at: www.ohchr.org/EN/HRBodies/UPR/Pages/MMindex.aspx

Human Rights Council (HRC). (2021b) *Resolution Adopted By the Human Rights Council on 14 July 2021, A/HRC/Res/47/24.* Available at: https://undocs.org/A/HRC/RES/47/24

Human Rights Council (HRC). (2021c) *Summary of the Stakeholders' Submissions on Myanmar, A/HRC/WG.6/37/MMR/3.* United Nations General Assembly. Available at: http://daccess-ods.un.org/access.nsf/Get?Open&DS=A/HRC/WG.6/37/MMR/3&Lang=E

Humphreys, David. (2017) Rights of Pachamama: The Emergence of an Earth Jurisprudence in the Americas. *Journal of International Relations & Development* 20(2017): 459–484.

Igoe, Jim. (2006) Becoming Indigenous Peoples: Difference, Inequality, & the Globalization of East African Identity Politics. *African Affairs* 105(240): 399–420.

Indigenous & Community Conserved Conservation Areas Consortium (ICCA Consortium). (2021) *The Fight for the Forest: Indigenous Peoples in Burma Speak Out on Threats Following the February Military Coup.* Available at: www.iccaconsortium.org/index.php/2021/11/12/the-fight-for-the-forest-indigenous-peoples-in-burma-speak-out-on-threats-following-the-february-military-coup/?fbclid=IwAR3f5rR_3Tfo12TlswZmI3DcSl7JzZzOQg4lHO 3DeU6VbngKCeuCl9roNdA

Indigenous Peoples/Ethnic Nationalities Network (IPEN). (2017) *Statement of Myanmar Indigenous Peoples/Ethnic Nationalities Network on the Occasion of the 23rd International Day of the World's Indigenous Peoples.* POINT. Available at: www.pointmyanmar.org/en/news/statement-myanmar-indigenous-peoplesethnic-nationalities-network-occasion-23rd-international

Institute for Global Environmental Strategies (IGES). (2021) *Study on Cooperative MRV as a Foundation for a Potential Regional Carbon Market within ASEAN: Myanmar Country Report.* Available at: https://unfccc.int/sites/default/files/resource/Myanmar%20country%20report%20Final.pdf

Institute for Human Rights and Business (IHRB). (2015) *Submission to the United Nations Human Rights Council Universal Periodic Review Session 23: Myanmar.* Institute for Human Rights and Business. Available at: www.ihrb.org/pdf/submissions/2015-UPR-Myanmar.pdf

International Commission of Jurists (ICJ). (2015) *International Commission of Jurists' (ICJ) Submission to the Universal Periodic Review of the Republic of the Union of Myanmar.* International Commission of Jurists. Available at: http://icj.wpengine.netdna-cdn.com/wp-content/uploads/2015/03/Myanmar-UPR-Advocacy-2015-ENG.pdf

International Covenant on Civil & Political Rights (ICCPR). (1966) Office of the High Commissioner for Human Rights. Available at: www.ohchr.org/en/professionalinterest/pages/ccpr.aspx

International Covenant on Economic, Social, & Cultural Rights (ICESCR). (1966) Office of the High Commissioner for Human Rights. Available at: www.ohchr.org/en/professionalinterest/pages/cescr.aspx

International Crisis Group (ICG). (2021) *Taking Aim at the Tatmadaw: The New Armed Resistance to Myanmar's Coup.* June 28, 2021. Available at: www.crisisgroup.org/asia/south-east-asia/myanmar/b168-taking-aim-tatmadaw-new-armed-resistance-myanmars-coup

International Fund for Agricultural Development (IFAD). (2021) *Indigenous Peoples' Forum.* Available at: www.ifad.org/en/indigenous-peoples-forum

International Indigenous Forum on Biodiversity (IIFB). (2012) *Convention on Biological Diversity (CBD).* Available at: https://iifb-fiib.org/[CE: link has changed to https://iifb-indigenous.org/]

International Indigenous Peoples' Forum on Climate Change (IIPFCC). (2021) *Who We Are.* Available at: www.iipfcc.org/who-are-we

International Labor Organization (ILO). (2017) *Indigenous Peoples & Climate Change: From Victims to Change Agents Through Decent Work.* Available at: www.ilo.org/global/topics/indigenous-tribal/WCMS_551189/lang--en/index.htm

International Labor Organization (ILO). (2019) *Implementing the ILO Indigenous & Tribal Peoples Convention No. 169: Towards an Inclusive, Sustainable, & Just Future.* Available at: www.ilo.org/wcmsp5/groups/public/---dgreports/---dcomm/---publ/documents/publication/wcms_735607.pdf

International Labor Organization (ILO). (2021a) *Ratifications of C169 – —Indigenous & Tribal Peoples Convention, 1989 (No. 169).* Available at: www.ilo.org/dyn/normlex/en/f?p=1000:11300:0::NO:11300:P11300_INSTRUMENT_ID:312314

International Labor Organization (ILO). (2021b) *Burma Citizenship Law 1982.* Available at: www.ilo.org/dyn/natlex/natlex4.detail?p_lang=en&p_isn=87413&p_country=MMR&p_count=86

International Labor Organization No. 169 (ILO No. 169). (1989) *Indigenous & Tribal Peoples Convention.* International Labor Organization. Available at: www.ilo.org/dyn/normlex/en/f?p=NORMLEXPUB:12100:0::NO::P12100_ILO_CODE:C169

International Work Group for Indigenous Affairs (IWGIA). (2011) *The Indigenous World.* International Work Group for Indigenous Affairs. Available at: www.iwgia.org/publications/search-pubs?publication_id=454

International Work Group for Indigenous Affairs (IWGIA). (2015) *The Universal Periodic Review.* International Work Group for Indigenous Affairs. Available at: www.iwgia.org/human-rights/un-mechanisms-and-processes/universal-periodic-review-upr

International Work Group for Indigenous Affairs (IWGIA). (2019a) *Collaboration for Coherence in Myanmar Climate Change Response.* Available at: www.google.com/url?sa=t&rct=j&q=&esrc=s&source=web&cd=&cad=rja&uact=8&ved=2ahUKEwijipm-ydX0AhUTSmwGHR3ZBd4QFnoECAcQAQ&url=https%3A%2F%2Fwww.iwgia.org%2Fen%2Fresources%2Fpublications%2F305-books%2F4401-the-necessity-collaboration-for-coherence-in-myanmar-climate-change-response.html&usg=AOvVaw3HavvbK1Cap3LQzRZgWFjU

International Work Group for Indigenous Affairs (IWGIA). (2019b) *Do Indigenous Peoples Hold the Key to Ssaving Myanmar's Remaining Forest?.* Available at: www.iwgia.org/en/climate-action/3310-do-indigenous-peoples-save-myanmars-forest.html

International Work Group for Indigenous Affairs (IWGIA). (2020a) *Indigenous People & Land Rights in Myanmar.* Available at: www.iwgia.org/en/myanmar/3904-indigenous-peoples-and-land-rights-in-myanmar.html

International Work Group for Indigenous Affairs (IWGIA). (2020b) *Indigenous Peoples Call for Climate Action Amidst Global Pandemic.* Available at: https://iwgia.org/en/news/3871-unfccc-joint-submission-aipp-iwgia.html

International Work Group for Indigenous Affairs (IWGIA). (2021a) Available at: https://iwgia.org/en/

International Work Group for Indigenous Affairs (IWGIA). (2021b) *Partners.* Available at: https://iwgia.org/en/iwgia-partners.html

Interview, pseudonym (Interview Pwe-zay X). (2021)

Interview, pseudonym (Interview Pwe-zay Y). (2021)

Interview, pseudonym (Interview Pwe-zay Z). (2021)

Ivison, Duncan. (2006) Emergent Cosmopolitanism: Indigenous Peoples & International Law, in Ronald Tinnevelt & Gert Verschraegen (eds.), *Between Cosmopolitan Ideals & State Sovereignty.* Springer.

James, Nickolas. (2018) Law & Power: Ten Lessons from Foucault. *Bond Law Review* 30(1): 4. Available at: https://pure.bond.edu.au/ws/portalfiles/portal/27624577/Law_and_Power_Ten_Lessons_From_Foucault.pdf

Jolliffe, Kim. (2015) *Ethnic Armed Conflict & Territorial Administration in Myanmar.* Asia Foundation. Available at: https://themimu.info/sites/themimu.info/files/documents/Report_Ethnic_Armed_Conflict_Territorial_Administration_in_Myanmar_TSF_Jul2015_ENG.pdf

Jorgensen, Miriam (ed.) (2007) *Rebuilding Native Nations: Strategies for Governance & Development.* University of Arizona Press.

Joseph, Brian. (2012) Political Transition in Burma: Four Scenarios in the Run-up to the 2015 Elections. *SAIS Review* 32(2): 137–149.

Jull, Janet, Melody Morton-Ninomiya, Irene Compton, & Annie Picard. (2018) Fostering the Conduct of Ethical & Equitable Research Practices: The Imperative for Integrated Knowledge Translation in Research Conducted By & with Indigenous Community Members. *Research Involvement & Engagement* 4(2018): 45–54.

Karlsson, Bengt. (2001) Indigenous Politics: Community Formation & Indigenous Peoples' Struggle for Self-Determination in Northeast India. *Identities* 8(1): 7–45.

Karlsson, Bengt. (2003) Anthropology & the "Indigenous Slot": Claims to & Debates about Indigenous Peoples' Status in India. *Critique of Anthropology* 23(4): 403–423.

Keating, Neal. (2016) Kites in the Highlands: Articulating Bunong Indigeneity in Cambodia, Vietnam, & Abroad. *Asian Ethnicity* 17(4): 566–579.

Keck, Margaret & Kathryn Sikkink. (1998) *Activists Beyond Borders: Advocacy Networks in International Politics.* Cornell University Press.

Kenrick, Justin. (2006) The Concept of Indigeneity. *Social Anthropology* 14(1): 17–32.

Khagram, Sanjeev, James Riker, & Kathryn Sikkink (eds.). (2002) *Restructuring World Politics: Transnational Social Movements, Networks, & Norms.* University of Minnesota Press.

Khan, Sabaa Ahmad. (2019) Rebalancing State & Indigenous Sovereignties in International Law: An Arctic Lens on Trajectories for Global Governance. *Leiden Journal of International Law* 32(4): 675–693.

Khan, Tauhid & Ellen MacEachen. (2021) Foucauldian Discourse Analysis: Moving Beyond a Social Constructionist Analytic. *International Journal of Qualitative Methods* 20(2021). Available at: https://doi.org/10.1177/16094069211018009

Kiersey, Nicholas & Doug Stokes. (2013) *Foucault & International Relations.* Routledge.

Kingsbury, Benedict. (1998) Indigenous Peoples in International Law: A Constructivist Approach to the Asian Controversy. *American Journal of International Law* 92(3): 414–457.

Klotz, Audie & Cecelia Lynch. (2014) *Strategies for Research in Constructivist International Relations.* Taylor & Francis.

Knauss, Stefan. (2018) Conceptualizing Human Stewardship in the Anthropocene: The Rights of Nature in Ecuador, New Zealand, & India. *Journal of Agricultural & Environmental Ethics* 31(2018): 703–722.

Koons, Judith. (2012) At the Tipping Point: Defining an Earth Jurisprudence for Social & Ecological Justice. *Loyola Law Review* 58(2): 349–390.

Koot, Stasja. (2020) Articulations of Inferiority: From Pre-Colonial to Post-Colonial Paternalism in Tourism & Development Among the Indigenous Bushmen of Southern Africa. *History & Anthropology.* Available at: www. tandfonline.com/doi/full/10.1080/02757206.2020.1830387

Kovach, Margaret. (2021) *Indigenous Methodologies: Characteristics, Conversations, & Contexts.* University of Toronto Press.

Kramer, Tom. (2015) Ethnic Conflict & Lands Rights in Myanmar. *Social Research* 82(2): 355–374.

Krech III, Shepard. (1999) *The Ecological Indian: Myth & History.* W.W. Norton & Company.

Krovel, Roy. (2018) Indigenous Perspectives on Researching Indigenous Peoples. *Social Identities* 24(1): 58–65.

Kuper, Adam. (2003) The Return of the Native. *Current Anthropology* 44(3): 389–402.

Kuyper, Jonathan, Bjorn-Ola Linner, & Heike Schroeder. (2018) Non-state Actors in Hybrid Global Climate Governance: Justice, Legitimacy, & Effectiveness in a Post-Paris Era. *WIREs Climate Change* 9(2018): 1–18.

LaDuke, Winona. (1983) Natural to Synthetic & Back Again, in W. Churchill (ed.), *Marxism and Native Americans.* South End Press.

Leepreecha, Prasit. (2019) Becoming Indigenous Peoples in Thailand. *Journal of Southeast Asian Studies* 50(1): 32–50.

Leifeld, Philip. (2020) Policy Debates & Discourse Network Analysis: A Research Agenda. *Politics & Governance* 8(2): 180–183.

Lennox, Connie & Damien Short (eds.). (2016) *Handbook of Indigenous Peoples' Rights.* Routledge.

Lenzerini, Federico. (2006) Sovereignty Revisited: International Law & Parallel Sovereignty of Indigenous Peoples. *Texas International Law Journal* 42(1): 155–190.

Lenzerini, Federico. (2019) Implementation of the UNDRIP Around the World: Achievements & Future Perspectives. *The International Journal of Human Rights* 23(1–2): 51–62.

Levi, Jerome & Bjorn Maybury-Lewis. (2012) Becoming Indigenous: Identity and Heterogeneity in a Global Movement, in Gillette Hall & Harry Patrinos (eds.), *Indigenous Peoples, Poverty, & Development*. 73–117. Cambridge University Press.

Li, Tania Murray. (2000) Articulating Indigenous Identity in Indonesia: Resource Politics & the Tribal Slot. *Comparative Studies in Society & History* 41(1): 149–179.

Li, Tania Murray. (2002) Ethnic Cleansing, Recursive Knowledge, & the Dilemmas of Sedentarism. *International Social Science Journal* 54(2002) 361–371.

Lightfoot, Sheryl. (2016) *Global Indigenous Politics*. Routledge.

Liljeblad, Jonathan. (2018) Beyond Transnational Advocacy: Lessons from Engagement of Myanmar Indigenous Peoples with the UN Human Rights Council Universal Periodic Review. *Vermont Law Review* 43(2): 217–250.

Liljeblad, Jonathan. (2022) "Virulent Pandemic & Fragile Democracy in Myanmar: Complications of COVID-19 Policies & the 2020 National Elections." *Australian Journal of Asian Law*. Forthcoming.

Liljeblad, Jonathan. (2023) International Human Rights Teachers in Myanmar Universities: The Individual Constraints of Structure on Intermediaries. *Journal of Human Rights*. Forthcoming.

Liljeblad, Jonathan & Bas Verschuuren. (2019) *Indigenous Perspectives on Sacred Natural Sites: Culture, Governance, & Conservation*. Routledge.

Liljeblad, Jonathan, Su Yin Htun, Po Po Maung, William Schulte. (2021) Chapter 51A: Environmental Law of Myanmar (Prior to the Military Coup of 1 February 2021), in Elizabeth Burleson, Lin-Heng Lye, & Nicholas Robinson (eds.), *Comparative Environmental Law & Regulation*. 1110–1179. Thomson Reuters.

Lindroth, Marjo. (2006) Indigenous-State Relations in the UN: Establishing the Indigenous Forum. *Polar Record* 42(3): 239–248.

Local Communities & Indigenous Peoples Platform (LCIPP). (2019a) *Initial Workplan (2020–2021) of the Local Communities & Indigenous Peoples Platform*. Available at: https://lcipp.unfccc.int/lcipp-background/2020-2021-workplan https://unfccc.int/sites/default/files/resource/Initial%20two-year%20workplan%20of%20the%20LCIPP%20%282020-2021%29.pdf

Local Communities & Indigenous Peoples Platform (LCIPP). (2019b) *Summary Report: Report of the Thematic In-Session Workshop: Enhancing the Participation of Local Communities, in Addition to Indigenous Peoples, in the Local Communities & Indigenous Peoples Platform*. Available at: https://unfccc.int/sites/default/files/resource/LCIPP%20workshop%20report_2019.pdf

Local Communities & Indigenous Peoples Platform (LCIPP). (2021) *United Nations Framework Convention on Climate Change (UNFCCC)*. Available at: https://unfccc.int/LCIPP#eq-2

Lupien, Pascal. (2020) Indigenous Movements, Collective Action, & Social Media: New Opportunities or New Threats? *Social Media + Society* 6(2): 1–11.

Lutz, Ellen. (2007) Indigenous Rights & the UN. *Anthropology News* 48(2): 28.

Macklem, Patrick. (2008) Indigenous Recognition in International Law: Theoretical Observations. *Michigan Journal of International Law* 30(1): 177–210.

Macpherson, Ian. (2016) An Analysis of Power in Transnational Advocacy Networks in Education, in Karen Mundy, in Andy Green, Bob Lingard, & Antoni Verger (eds.), *Handbook of Global Education Policy*. 401–418. Wiley.

Manuel, George & Michael Posluns. (1974) *The Fourth World: An Indian Reality*. Collier Macmillan.

Martin, Pamela. (2003) *The Globalization of Contentious Politics: The Amazonian Indigenous Rights Movement*. Routledge.

Martin, Pamela. (2011) Global Governance from the Amazon: Leaving Oil Underground in Yasuni National Park, Ecuador. *Global Environmental Politics* 11(4): 22–42.

Martin, Pamela & Franke Wilmer. (2017) Normative Struggles & Globalization: The Case of Indigenous Peoples in Bolivia & Ecuador, in Michael Stohl, Mark Lichbach, & Peter Grabosky (eds.), *States & People in Conflict*. 340–379. Routledge.

Martinez-Torres, Maria Elena & Peter Rosset. (2010) La Via Campesina: The Birth & Evolution of a Transnational Social Movement. *The Journal of Peasant Studies* 37(1): 149–175.

McAteer, Emily & Simone Pulver. (2009) The Corporate Boomerang: Shareholder Transnational Advocacy Networks Targeting Oil Companies in the Ecuadorian Amazon. *Global Environmental Politics* 9(1): 1–30.

McFarlane, Colin. (2006) Transnational Development Networks: Bringing Development & Postcolonial Approaches into Dialogue. *The Geographical Journal* 172(1): 35–49.

McIntyre-Tamwoy, Susan, Maureen Fuary, & Alice Buhrich. (2013) Understanding Climate, Adapting to Change: Indigenous Cultural Values & Climate Change Impacts in North Queensland. *Local Environment* 18(1): 91–109.

McKeown, Ryder. (2017) International Law & Its Discontents: Exploring the Dark Sides of International Law in International Relations. *Review of International Studies* 43(3): 430–452.

Mengden, Walter. (2017) Indigenous People, Human Rights, & Consultation: The Dakota Access Pipeline. *American Indian Law Review* 41(2): 441–466.

Mercado, Antonieta. (2011) *Grassroots Cosmopolitanism: Transnational Communication & Citizenship Practices Among Indigenous Mexican Immigrants in the United States*. Dissertation, University of California San Diego. Proquest.

Merlan, Francesca. (2009) Indigeneity: Global & Local. *Currently Anthropology* 50(3): 303–333.

Merry, Sally. (2006) *Human Rights & Gender Violence: Translating International Law into Local Justice*. University of Chicago Press.

Mills, Sara. (2004) *Discourse*. Routledge.

Minami, Daisuke. (2018) Lost in Translation: Problematizing the Localization of Transnational Activism. *European Journal of International Relations* 25(2): 511–537.

Ministry of Natural Resources & Environmental Conservation (MoNREC). (2015) *Myanmar's Intended National Determined Contribution-INDC*.

Available at: https://www4.unfccc.int/sites/ndcstaging/PublishedDocuments/ Myanmar%20First/Myanmar%27s%20INDC.pdf

Ministry of Natural Resources & Environmental Conservation (MoNREC). (2019a) *Myanmar Climate Change Policy*. Available at: https://unhabitat.org/ myanmar-climate-change-policy

Ministry of Natural Resources & Environmental Conservation (MoNREC). (2019b) *Myanmar Climate Change Strategy*. Available at: https://myanmar. un.org/sites/default/files/2019-11/MyanmarClimateChangeStrategy_2019.pdf

Ministry of Natural Resources & Environmental Conservation (MoNREC). (2019c) *Myanmar Climate Change Master Plan*. Available at: https:// unhabitat.org/sites/default/files/2019/10/mccmp_eng_ready-to-print_27- may-2019.pdf

Ministry of Natural Resources & Environmental Conservation (MoNREC). (2020a) *SCF Forum: Financing Nature Based Solutions, Proposal from the Union Government of the Republic of Myanmar*. Available at: https://unfccc. int/sites/default/files/resource/Myanmar-Draft_SW.pdf

Ministry of Natural Resources & Environmental Conservation (MoNREC). (2020b) *Myanmar's National Approach to REDD+ Safeguards*. Available at: https://unredd.net/documents/global-programme-191/safeguards-multiple- benefits-297/studies-reports-and-publications-1/17414-myanmars-national- approach-to-redd-safeguards-eng.html

Ministry of Natural Resources & Environmental Conservation (MoNREC). (2021) *Myanmar National Determined Contributions*. Available at: www4. unfccc.int/sites/ndcstaging/PublishedDocuments/Myanmar%20First/ Myanmar%20Updated%20%20NDC%20July%202021.pdf

Miranda, Lillian Aponte. (2010) Indigenous Peoples as International Lawmakers. *University of Pennsylvania Journal of International Law* 32(2010): 203–263.

Mitchell, Derek. (2013) Burma's Challenge. *Fletcher Forum of World Affairs* 37(3): 13–20.

Moon, Suerie. (2019) Power in Global Governance: An Expanded Typology from Global Health. *Globalization & Health* 15(2019). Available at: https:// doi.org/10.1186/s12992-019-0515-5

Morgan, Rhiannon. (2007) On Political Institutions & Social Movement Dynamics: The Case of the United Nations & the Global Indigenous Movement. *International Political Science Review* 28(3): 273–292.

Morton, Micah. (2017) Indigenous Peoples Work to Raise Their Status in Reforming Myanmar. *ISEAS Perspective* 2017(33). Available at: www.iseas. edu.sg/images/pdf/ISEAS_Perspective_2017_33.pdf

Morton, Micah & Ian Baird. (2019) From Hill Tribes to Indigenous Peoples: The Localisation of a Global Movement in Thailand. *Journal of Southeast Asian Studies* 50(1): 7–31.

Morton, Micah, Jianhua Wang, & Haiying Li. (2016) Decolonizing Methods: Akha Articulations of Indigeneity in the Upper Mekong Region. *Asian Ethnicity* 17(4): 580–595.

Muehlebach, Andrea. (2001) "Making Place" at the United Nations: Indigenous Cultural Politics at the U.N. Working Group on Indigenous Populations. *Cultural Anthropology* 16(3): 415–448.

Muller, A. (2015) Using Discourse Analysis to Measure Discourse Coalitions: Towards a Formal Analysis of Political Discourse. *World Political Science* 11(2015): 377–404.

Mundy, Karen & Lynn Murphy. (2001) Transnational Advocacy, Global Civil Society? Emerging Evidence from the Field of Education. *Comparative Education Review* 45(1): 85–126.

Murray, Jamie. (2014) Earth Jurisprudence, Wild Law, Emergent Law: The Emerging Field of Ecology & Law—Part 1. *Liverpool Law Review* 35(2014): 215–231.

Murray, Jamie. (2015) Earth Jurisprudence, Wild Law, Emergent Law: The Emerging Field of Ecology & Law—Part 2. *Liverpool Law Review* 36(2015): 105–122.Myanmar Constitution. (2008) *Myanmar Constitution.* Available at: www.burmalibrary.org/docs5/Myanmar_Constitution-2008-en. pdf

Myint, Moe. (2017) Analysis: Tug of War Over Indigenous Rights & Government's Forestry Plan, December 4, 2017. *The Irrawaddy.* Available at: www.irrawaddy.com/news/burma/tug-war-indigenous-rights-govts-forestry-plan.html

Myint-U, Thant. (2001) *The Making of Modern Burma.* Cambridge University Press.

Nagoya Protocol. (2010) *Nagoya Protocol on Access & Benefit-Sharing.* Available at: www.cbd.int/abs/

Nah, Alice. (2003) Negotiating Indigenous Identity in Postcolonial Malaysia: Beyond Being "Not Quite/Not Malay." *Social Identities* 9(4): 511–534.

Nakamura, Naohiro. (2015) Being Indigenous in a Non-Indigenous Environment: Identity Politics of the Dogai Ainu & the New Indigenous Policies of Japan. *Environment & Planning* 47(2015): 660–675.

Nakanishi, Yoshinori. (2013) *Strong Soldiers, Failed Revolution.* National University of Singapore Press.

National Land Use Policy (NLUP). (2016) *Myanmar National Land Use Policy 2016.* Available at: www.burmalibrary.org/en/myanmar-national-land-use-policy-english

Nettelbeck, Amanda. (2019) *Indigenous Rights & Colonial Subjecthood.* Cambridge University Press.

Niezen, Ronald. (2003) *The Origins of Indigenism: Human Rights & the Politics of Identity.* University of California Press.

Niezen, Ronald. (2009) *The Rediscovered Self: Indigenous Identity & Cultural Justice.* McGill-Queen's University Press.Nixon, Hamish, et al. (2013) *State and Region Governments in Myanmar. Asia Foundation.* Available at: https://asiafoundation.org/resources/pdfs/StateandRegionGovernmentsinMyanmarCESDTAF.PDF

Noakes, Stephen. (2012) Transnational Advocacy Networks and Moral Commitment: The Free Tibet Campaign Meets the Chinese State. *International Journal* 67(2): 507–525.

Noisecat, Julian Brave. (2016) Slaying the Carbon-Consuming Colonial Hydra: Indigenous Contributions to Climate Action. *Development* 59(2016): 199–204.

Nugent, Stephen. (2009) *Indigenism & Cultural Authenticity in Brazilian Amazonia*. University College of London.

Nyein, Nyein. (2020) This Is Our Land—And That's the Truth: Pa-O Farmers Challenge Myanmar Military, June 10, 2020. *The Irrawaddy*. Available at: www.irrawaddy.com/news/burma/land-thats-truth-pa-o-farmers-challenge-myanmar-military.html

O'Donnell, Erin, Anne Poelina, Alessandro Pelizzon, & Cristy Clark. (2020) Stop Burying the Lede: The Essential Role of Indigenous Law(s) in Creating Rights of Nature. *Transnational Environmental Law* 9(3): 403–427.

Office of the High Commissioner for Human Rights (OHCHR). (2012) *Statement of High Commissioner for Human Rights Navi Pillay at the UNEP World Congress on Justice, Governance & Law for Environmental Sustainability*. Available at: https://newsarchive.ohchr.org/EN/NewsEvents/Pages/DisplayNews.aspx?NewsID=12263&LangID=e

Office of the High Commissioner for Human Rights (OHCHR). (2018) *Framework Principles on Human Rights & the Environment*. Available at: www.ohchr.org/Documents/Issues/Environment/SREnvironment/FrameworkPrinciplesUserFriendlyVersion.pdf

Office of the High Commissioner for Human Rights (OHCHR). (2019) *Country Engagement Mission (8–13 April 2019) – —New Zealand Advisory Note*. Available at: www.tpk.govt.nz/documents/download/6305/EMRIPAdvisroyNoteNZ2019.pdf

Office of the High Commissioner for Human Rights (OHCHR). (2020) *Technical Advisory Note – —Repatriation Request for the Yaqui Maaso Kova*. Available at: www.ohchr.org/Documents/Issues/IPeoples/EMRIP/Session12/MaasoKova.pdf

Office of the High Commissioner for Human Rights' (OHCHR). (2021a) *Basic Facts about the UPR*. Available at: www.ohchr.org/EN/HRBodies/UPR/Pages/BasicFacts.aspx

Office of the High Commissioner for Human Rights (OHCHR). (2021b) *Cycles of the Universal Periodic Review*. Available at: www.ohchr.org/EN/HRBodies/UPR/Pages/MMIndex.aspx

Office of the High Commissioner for Human Rights (OHCHR). (2021c) *Universal Periodic Review—Myanmar*. Available at: www.ohchr.org/EN/HRBodies/UPR/Pages/CyclesUPR.aspx

Office of the High Commissioner for Human Rights (OHCHR). (2021d) *Special Rapporteur on the Situation of Human Rights in Myanmar*. Available at: www.ohchr.org/en/hrbodies/sp/countriesmandates/mm/pages/srmyanmar.aspx

Office of the High Commissioner for Human Rights (OHCHR). (2021e) *Open Letter to Senior General Min Aung Hlaing*. Available at: www.ohchr.org/Documents/Countries/MM/Open-letter-SR-Myanmar.pdf

Office of the High Commissioner for Human Rights (OHCHR). (2021f) *Written Updates of the Office of the High Commissioner for Human Rights on the Situation of Human Rights in Myanmar, A/HRC/48/67.* Available at: www.ohchr.org/EN/HRBodies/HRC/RegularSessions/Session48/Pages/ListReports.aspx

Office of the High Commissioner for Human Rights (OHCHR). (2021g) *Integrating Human Rights at the UNFCCC.* Available at: www.ohchr.org/EN/Issues/HRAndClimateChange/Pages/UNFCCC.aspx

Office of the High Commissioner for Human Rights (OHCHR). (2021h) *The Impact of Climate Change on the Rights of People in Vulnerable Situations.* Available at: www.ohchr.org/EN/Issues/HRAndClimateChange/Pages/PeopleVulnerableSituations.aspx

Office of the High Commissioner for Human Rights (OHCHR). (2021i) *Special Rapporteur on Human Rights & the Environment.* Available at: www.ohchr.org/en/Issues/environment/SRenvironment/Pages/SRenvironmentIndex.aspx

Office of the High Commissioner for Human Rights (OHCHR). (2021j) *Special Rapporteur on the Rights of Indigenous Peoples.* Available at: www.ohchr.org/en/issues/ipeoples/srindigenouspeoples/pages/sripeoplesindex.aspx

Office of the High Commissioner for Human Rights (OHCHR). (2021k) *Rio+ 20 United Nations Conference on Sustainable Development.* Available at: www.ohchr.org/EN/NewsEvents/Rio20/Pages/Rio20Index.aspx

Office of the High Commissioner for Human Rights (OHCHR). (2021l) *Remarks By Thomas H. Andrews, UN Special Rapporteur on the Situation of Human Rights in Myanmar at the 76th Session of the General Assembly of the United Nations.* Available at: www.ohchr.org/en/NewsEvents/Pages/DisplayNews.aspx?NewsID=27696&LangID=E

Office of the High Commissioner for Human Rights (OHCHR). (2021m) *Written Updates of the Office of the High Commissioner for Human Rights on the Situation of Human Rights in Myanmar, A/HRC/48/67.* Available at: www.ohchr.org/EN/HRBodies/HRC/RegularSessions/Session48/Pages/ListReports.aspx

Ogburn, Dennis. (2008) Becoming Saraguro: Ethnogenesis in the Context of Inca & Spanish Colonialism. *Ethnohistory* 55(2): 287–319.

Ong, Andrew. (2021) Ethnic Armed Organizations in Post-Coup Myanmar: New Conversations Needed. *ISEAS Perspective* 79(2021). Available at: www.iseas.edu.sg/wp-content/uploads/2021/05/ISEAS_Perspective_2021_79.pdf

Oo, Aung Naing. (2015) Armed Conflict: The Beginning of the End. *Myanmar Times.* August 25, 2015. Available at: www.mmtimes.com/index.php/opinion/16137-armed-conflict-the-beginning-of-the-end.html

Ormaza, Maria Victoria Cabrera. (2012) Re-Thinking the Role of Indigenous Peoples in International Law: New Developments in International Environmental Law & Development Cooperation. *Goettingen Journal of International Law* 4(1): 243–270.

Ortiz, Laura Velasco & Margot Olavarria. (2014) Transnational Ethnic Processes: Indigenous Mexican Migration to the United States. *Latin American Perspectives* 41(3): 54–74.

Pahuja, Sundhya. (2005) The Postcoloniality of International Law. *Harvard International Law Journal* 46(2): 459–470.

Paredes, Oona. (2019) Preserving "Tradition": The Business of Indigeneity in the Modern Philippine Context. *Journal of Southeast Asian Studies* 50(1): 86–106.

Paudel, Dinesh. (2016) Ethnic Identity Politics in Nepal: Liberation from, or Restoration of, Elite Interest? *Asian Ethnicity* 17(4): 548–565.

Peace Research Institute Oslo (PRIO). (2021) *The New Pattern of Conflict in Myanmar*. December 1, 2021. Available at: https://blogs.prio.org/2021/12/the-new-pattern-of-conflict-in-myanmar/

Pearl, M. Alexander. (2018) Human Rights, Indigenous Peoples, & the Global Climate Crisis. *Wake Forest Law Review* 53(4): 713–738.

Peez, Anton. (2022) "Contributions & Blind Spots of Constructivist Norms Research in International Relations, 1980-2018: A Systematic Evidence & Gap Analysis." *International Studies Review* 24(1): https://doi.org/10.1093/isr/viab055.

Pelican, Michaela. (2015) *Masks & Staffs: Identity Politics in the Cameroon Grassfields*. Berghahn.

Pelican, Michaela. (2009) Complexities of Indigeneity & Autochthony: An African Example. *American Ethnologist* 36(1): 149–162.

Pelican, Michaela & Junko Maruyama. (2015) The Indigenous Rights Movement in Africa: Perspectives from Botswana & Cameroon. *African Study Monographs* 36(1): 49–74.

Phillips, James. (2015) The Rights of Indigenous Peoples Under International Law. *Global Bioethics* 26(2): 120–127.

Pitts, Jennifer. (2017) International Relations & the Critical History of International Law. *International Relations* 31(3): 282–298.

Poling, Gregory & Simon Trudes. (2021) *Myanmar's Military Seizes Power*. Center for Strategic & International Studies. Available at: www.csis.org/analysis/myanmars-military-seizes-power

Porath, Nathan. (2010) "They Have Not Progressed Enough": Development's Negated Identities Among Two Indigenous Peoples (*Orang Asli*) in Indonesia & Thailand. *Journal of Southeast Asian Studies* 41(2): 267–289.

Powless, Ben. (2012) An Indigenous Movement to Confront Climate Change. *Globalizations* 9(3): 411–424.

Poyer, Lin. (2017). World War II & the Development of Global Indigenous Identities. *Identities* 24(4): 417–435.

Progressive Voice. (2018) *Statement on the Opening of the Vacant, Fallow, & Virgin Land Management Central Committee for Applying VFV Lands*. Available at: https://progressivevoicemyanmar.org/2018/11/06/statement-on-the-opening-of-the-vacant-fallow-virgin-land-management-central-committee-for-applying-vfv-lands/

Promotion of Indigenous & Nature Together (POINT). (2015) Available at: www.point-myanmar.org/en_US/

Promotion of Indigenous & Nature Together (POINT). (2017) *Myanmar's Climate Change Commitments & Indigenous Peoples' Rights*. Available at: www.pointmyanmar.org/en/publication/myanmars-climate-change-commitments-and-indigenous-peoples-rights

Promotion of Indigenous & Nature Together (POINT). (2020) *Linking Climate Change & Sustainable Development in Myanmar*. Available at: www.pointmyanmar.org/en/publication/linking-climate-change-and-sustainable-development-myanmar

Puig, Sergio. (2019) International Indigenous Economic Law. *University of California Davis Law Review* 52(3): 1243–1316.

Radio Free Asia (RFA). (2021) *Myanmar's Junta Blocked from Attending Global Climate Summit, November 20, 2021*. Available at: www.rfa.org/english/news/myanmar/snubbed-11102021183951.html

Rasch, Elisabet. (2020) Becoming a Maya Woman: Beauty Pageants at the Intersection of Indigeneity, Gender, & Class in Quetzaltenango. *Guatemala. Journal of Latin American Studies* 52(2020): 133–156.

Risse, Thomas, Stephen Ropp, & Kathryn Sikkink. (1999) *The Power of Human Rights: International Norms and Domestic Change*. Cambridge University Press.

Rodrigues, Maria Guadalupe Moog. (2004) *Global Environmentalism and Local Politics: Transnational Advocacy Networks in Brazil, Ecuador, and India*. State University of New York Press.

Rodriguez-Garavito, Cesar. (2011) Ethnicity.gov: Global Governance, Indigenous Peoples, & the Right to Prior Consultation in Social Minefields. *Indiana Journal of Global Legal Studies* 18(1): 263–305.

Rodriguez-Garavito, Cesar & Luis Carlos Arenas. (2005) Indigenous Rights, Transnational Activism, & Legak Mobilization: The Struggle of the U'wa People in Colombia, in Boaventura de Sousa Santos & Cesar Rodriguez-Garavito (eds.), *Law & Globalization from Below*. Cambridge University Press.

Roth, Kenneth. (2004) Defending Economic, Social and Cultural Rights: Practice Issues Faced By an International Human Rights Organization. *Human Rights Quarterly* 26: 63–73.

Sanmuki, Miriam Harjati. (2013) Mobilities of Indigeneity: Intermediary NGOs & Indigenous Peoples in Indonesia, in Brigitta Hauser-Schaublin (ed.) *Adat & Indigeneity in Indonesia: Culture & Entitlements Between Heteronomy & Self-Ascription*. Gottingen University Press.

Sapignoli, Maria & Robert Hitchcock. (2013) Indigenous Peoples in Southern Africa. *The Round Table* 102(4): 355–365.

Sargent, Sarah. (2012) Transnational Networks & United Nations Human Rights Structural Change: The Future of Indigenous & Minority Rights. *The International Journal of Human Rights* 16(1): 123–151.

Saugestad, Sidsel. (2001) *The Inconvenient Indigenous: Remote Area Development in Botswana, Donor Assistance, & the First People of the Kalahari*. Nordiska Afrikainstitutet.

Saugestad, Sidsel. (2011) Impact of International Mechanisms on Indigenous Rights in Botswana. *International Journal of Human Rights* 15(1): 37–61.

Sawyer, Suzana. (2004) *Crude Chronicles: Indigenous Politics, Multinational Oil, and Neoliberalism in Ecuador*. Duke University Press.

Schillmoller, Anne & Alessandro Pelizzon. (2013) Mapping the Terrain of Earth Jurisprudence: Landscape, Thresholds, & Horizons. *Environmental & Earth Law Journal* 3(2013): 1–32.

Scholte, Jan Aart. (2002) Civil Society and Democracy in Global Governance. *Global Governance* 8(3): 281–306.

Shaw, Rhonda, Julie Howe, Jonathan Beazer, & Toni Carr. (2019) Ethics & Positionality in Qualitative Research with Marginal Groups. *Qualitative Research* 20(3): 277–293.

Sidorova, Evgeniia. (2019) Circumpolar Indigeneity in Canada, Russia, & the United States (Alaska): Do Differences Result in Representational Challenges for the Arctic Council? *Arctic* 71(1): 71–81.

Simpson, Leanne. (2008) Looking after Gdoo-naaganinaa: Precolonial Nishnaabeg Diplomatic & Treaty Relationships. *Wicazo Sa Review* 23(2): 29–42.

Sium, Aman, Chandnui Desai, & Eric Ritskes. (2012) Towards the "Tangible Unknown": Decolonization & the Indigenous Future. *Decolonization: Indigeneity, Education, & Society* 1(1): 1–13.

Sloan, Spencer. (2013) Accommodation & Rectification: A Dual Approach to Indigenous Peoples in International Law. *Columbia Journal of Transnational Law* 51(3): 739–775.

Smith, Linda Tuhiwai. (2007) *Decolonizing Methodologies: Research & Indigenous Peoples*. Zed Books Limited.

Smith, Will & Wolfram Dressler. (2020) Forged in Flames: Indigeneity, Forest Fire, & Geographies of Blame in the Philippines. *Postcolonial Studies* 23(4): 527–545.

Snaing, Yen. (2015) Indigenous Rights Coalition in Burma Plans UPR Submission. *The Irrawaddy, July 21, 2015*. Available at: www.irrawaddy. org/burma/indigenous-rights-coalition-in-burma-plans-upr-submission. html

Solway, Jacqueline & Richard Lee. (1990) Foragers, Genuine or Spurious? Situating the Kalahari San in History. *Current Anthropology* 31(199): 109–146.

South, Ashley. (2008) *Ethnic Politics in Burma: States of Conflict*. Routledge.

Sperling, Valerie, Mya Marx Ferree, & Barbara Risman. (2001) Constructing Global Feminism: Transnational Advocacy Networks and Russian Women's Activism. *Globalization and Gender* 26(4): 1155–1186.

Sprenger, Guido. (2013) Transcultural Communication & Social Order: Comparisons in Upland Southeast Asia. *Asian Ethnology* 72(2): 299–319.

Stavig, Ward. (2000) Ambiguous Visions: Nature, Law, & Culture in Indigenous-Spanish Land Relations in Colonial Peru. *The Hispanic American Historical Review* 80(1): 77–111.

Steinberg, David. (2010) *Burma/Myanmar: What Everyone Needs to Know*. Oxford University Press.

Survival International. (2021) *Terminology*. Available at: www.survival international.org/info/terminology

Swift, Peter. (2017). The Burma Democratic Front: How Eighty-Eight Generation Chin Were Mobilized into the Chin National Front. *Journal of Burma Studies* 21(1): 133–169.

Sylvain, Renee. (2002) "Land, Water, and Truth": San Identity and Global Indigenism. *American Anthropologist* 104(4): 1074–1085.

Tallbear, Kim. (2013) Genomic Articulations of Indigeneity. *Social Studies of Science* 43(4): 509–533.

Tamuno, Paul. (2017) New Human Rights Concept for Old African Problems: An Analysis of the Challenges of Introducing & Implementing Indigenous Rights in Africa. *Journal of African Law* 61(3): 305–332.

Tan, Rhe-Anne. (2020) "We Are Not Red & White, We Are Morning Star!" Internal Colonization, Indigenous Identity, & the Idea of Indonesia. *Politics of Protest* 73(2): 271–284.

Tarrow, Sidney. (2005) *The New Transnational Activism*. Cambridge University Press.

Taylor, Robert. (2009) *The State in Myanmar*. Hurst Publishers.

Taylor, Robert. (2015) Refighting Old Battles, Compounding Misconceptions: The Politics of Ethnicity in Myanmar Today. *ISEAS Perspective* 2015(12). Available at: www.burmalibrary.org/sites/burmalibrary.org/files/obl/docs21/Taylor-2015-iseas_perspective-red.pdf

Teran, Maria Yolanda. (2016) The Nagoya Protocol & Indigenous Peoples. *The International Indigenous Policy Journal* 7(2). Available at: https://ir.lib.uwo.ca/iipj/vol7/iss2/6/

Thawnghmung, Ardeth Maung. (2016) The Politics of Indigeneity in Myanmar: Competing Narratives in Rakhine State. *Asian Ethnicity* 17(4): 527–547.

The Guardian. (2021a) Myanmar Army Chiefs Order Arrest of Leading Coup Opponents. *The Guardian*, 14 February 2021. Available at: www.theguardian.com/world/2021/feb/13/myanmar-army-chiefs-order-arrest-of-leading-coup-opponents

The Guardian. (2021b) Myanmar Coup: Civil Disobedience Campaign Begins Amid Calls for Aung San Suu Kyi's Release. *The Guardian*, 3 February 2021. Available at: www.theguardian.com/global-development/2021/feb/02/myanmar-coup-military-tightens-grip-amid-calls-for-suu-kyi-to-be-freed

The Guardian. (2021c) Myanmar Coup: Who Are the Military Figures Running the Country? *The Guardian*, 2 February 2021. Available at: www.theguardian.com/world/2021/feb/02/myanmar-coup-who-are-the-military-figures-running-the-country

The Guardian. (2021d) The Army Takes Power in Coup as Aung San Suu Kyi Detained. *The Guardian*, 1 February 2021. Available at: www.theguardian.com/world/2021/feb/01/aung-san-suu-kyi-and-other-figures-detained-in-myanmar-raids-says-ruling-party

Theriault, Noah. (2019) Unravelling the Strings Attached: Philippine Indigeneity in Law & Practice. *Journal of Southeast Asian Studies* 50(1): 107–128.

Thobani, Sunera. (2008) Reading TWAIL in the Canadian Context: Race, Gender, & National Formation. *International Community Law Review* 10(2008): 421–430.

Tilley, Virginia. (2002) New Help or New Hegemony? The Transnational Indigenous Peoples' Movement & "Being Indian" in El Salvador. *Journal of Latin American Studies* 34(3): 525–554.

Tilly, Charles & Sidney Tarrow. (2015) *Contentious Politics, 2nd Edition.* Oxford University Press.

Timperley, Claire. (2020) Constellations of Indigeneity: The Power of Definition. *Contemporary Political Theory* 19(1): 38–60.

Tohring, S.R. (2010) *Violence & Identity in North-East India.* Mittal Publications.

Tran, Van. (2021). *Myanmar's Military Has a History of Deceptive Tactics Against Protesters. Now It Has Social Media, Too, February 20, 2021.* Available at: www.washingtonpost.com/politics/2021/02/10/myanmars-military-has-history-using-deceptive-tactics-against-protesters-now-it-has-social-media-too/

Transparency International. (2020) *Myanmar.* Available at: www.transparency.org/en/countries/myanmar

Tridgell, Jennifer. (2016) Seeing REDD: Carbon Forest Programmes & Indigenous Rights. *Australian Journal of Environmental* Law 2016 (2016): 86–94.

Trubek, David, Jim Mosher, & Jeffrey Rothstein. (2000) Transnationalism in the Regulation of Labor Relations: International Regimes and Transnational Advocacy Networks. *Law & Social Inquiry* 25(4): 1187–1211.

Tsing, Anna. (2007) Indigenous Voice, in Marisol de la Cadena & Orin Starn (eds.), *Indigenous Experience Today.* 31–67. Routledge.

Tsosie, Rebecca. (2010) Indigenous Peoples & Global Climate Change: Intercultural Models of Climate Equity. *Journal of Environmental Law & Litigation* 25(1): 7–18.

Turner, Dale. (2006) *This Is Not a Peace Pipe: Towards a Critical Indigenous Philosophy.* University of Toronto Press.

Uddin, Nasir. (2019) The Local Translation of Global Indigeneity: A Case of the Chittagong Hill Tracts. *Journal of Southeast Asian Studies* 50(1): 68–85.

Uddin, Nasir, Eva Gerharz, & Pradeep Chakkarath. (2017). *Indigeneity on the Move: Varying Manifestations of a Contested Concept.* Berghahn Books.

United Nations (UN). (2021a) *Indigenous Peoples at the United Nations.* United Nations. Available at: www.un.org/development/desa/indigenouspeoples/about-us.html

United Nations (UN). (2021b) *Permanent Forum.* United Nations. Available at: www.un.org/development/desa/indigenouspeoples/unpfii-sessions-2.html

United Nations (UN). (2021c) *Special Rapporteur on the Rights of Indigenous Peoples. Office of the High Commissioner for Human Rights.* Available at: www.ohchr.org/EN/Issues/IPeoples/SRIndigenousPeoples/Pages/SRIPeoplesIndex.aspx

United Nations (UN). (2021d) *UN Treaty Body Database.* Available at: https://tbinternet.ohchr.org/_layouts/15/TreatyBodyExternal/Treaty.aspx?CountryID=119&Lang=EN

United Nations (UN). (2021e) *United Nations Climate Change.* Available at: https://unfccc.int/node/61122

United Nations (UN). (2021f) *United Nations Treaty Database: United Nations Framework Convention on Climate Change 1992.* Available at: https://treaties.un.org/Pages/ViewDetailsIII.aspx?src=IND&mtdsg_no=XXVII-7&chapter=27&Temp=mtdsg3&clang=_en

United Nations Conference on Environment & Development (UNCED). (1992) *United Nations General Assembly A/CONF.151/26.* Available at: www.un.org/en/development/desa/population/migration/generalassembly/docs/globalcompact/A_CONF.151_26_Vol.I_Declaration.pdf

United Nations Declaration on the Rights of Indigenous Peoples (UNDRIP). (2007) *United Nations.* Available at: www.ilo.org/dyn/normlex/en/f?p=NORMLEXPUB:12100:0::NO::P12100_ILO_CODE:C169

United Nations Development Program (UNDP). (2020) *Human Development Report 2020.* United Nations Development Program. Available at: http://hdr.undp.org/en/2020-report

United Nations Framework Convention on Climate Change (UNFCCC). (2005) *Decision 27/CMP.1 Procedures & Mechanisms Relating to Compliance Under the Kyoto Protocol.* Available at: https://unfccc.int/files/kyoto_protocol/compliance/application/pdf/dec.27_cmp.1.pdf

United Nations Framework Convention on Climate Change (UNFCCC). (2010) *Report of the Conference of the Parties on Its Sixteenth Session, Held in Cancun from 29 November to 10 December 2010, FCCC/CP/2010/7/Add.1.* Available at: https://unfccc.int/resource/docs/2010/cop16/eng/07a01.pdf

United Nations Framework Convention on Climate Change (UNFCCC). (2012) *Myanmar's Initial Communication Under the United Nations Framework Convention on Climate Change (UNFCCC).* Ministry of Environmental Conservation & Forestry. Available at: https://unfccc.int/sites/default/files/resource/mmrnc1.pdf

United Nations Framework Convention on Climate Change (UNFCCC). (2015) *Paris Agreement.* Available at: https://unfccc.int/sites/default/files/english_paris_agreement.pdf

United Nations Framework Convention on Climate Change (UNFCCC). (2019a) *Summary Report: Partnership-Building Dialogue on Work Outside of the Convention Relevant to the Local Communities & Indigenous Peoples Platform.* Available at: https://unfccc.int/sites/default/files/resource/SR-Partnership-building_final.pdf

United Nations Framework Convention on Climate Change (UNFCCC). (2019b) *Report of the Conference of the Parties Serving as the Meeting of the Parties to the Paris Agreement on the Third Part of Its First Session, Held in Katowice from 2 to 15 December 2018, FCCC/PA/CMA/2018/3/*

Add.2. Available at: https://unfccc.int/sites/default/files/resource/CMA2018_03a02E.pdf

United Nations Framework Convention on Climate Change (UNFCCC). (2021) *Myanmar.* Available at: https://unfccc.int/node/61122

United Nations Framework Convention on Climate Change Admitted NGOs (UNFCCC Admitted NGOs). (2021) *Admitted NGOs.* Available at: https://unfccc.int/process/parties-non-party-stakeholders/non-party-stakeholders/admitted-ngos/list-of-admitted-ngos

United Nations Framework Convention on Climate Change Bodies (UNFCCC Bodies). (2021) *What Are Governing, Process Management, Subsidiary, Constituted, & Concluded Bodies?* Available at: https://unfccc.int/process-and-meetings/bodies/the-big-picture/what-are-governing-process-management-subsidiary-constituted-and-concluded-bodies

United Nations Framework Convention on Climate Change Documents (UNFCCC Documents). (2021) *Myanmar.* Available at: https://unfccc.int/documents?search2=&search3=myanmar

United Nations Framework Convention on Climate Change Global Stocktake (UNFCCC GST). (2021) *Global Stocktake.* Available at: https://unfccc.int/topics/global-stocktake

United Nations Framework Convention on Climate Change Non-Party Stakeholders (UNFCCC Stakeholders). (2021) *Overview.* Available at: https://unfccc.int/process-and-meetings/parties-non-party-stakeholders/non-party-stakeholders/overview

United Nations Framework Convention on Climate Change Observer Status (UNFCCC Observers). (2021) *How to Obtain Observer Status.* Available at: https://unfccc.int/process-and-meetings/parties-non-party-stakeholders/non-party-stakeholders/overview/how-to-obtain-observer-status

United Nations Framework Convention on Climate Change REDD+ (UNFCCC REDD+). (2019) *Report of the Technical Assessment of the Proposed Forest Reference Level of Myanmar Submitted in 2018, FCCC/TAW/2018/MMR.* Available at: https://unfccc.int/sites/default/files/resource/tar2018_MMR.pdf

United Nations Framework Convention on Climate Change REDD+ (UNFCCC REDD+). (2021a) *What Is REDD+?* Available at: https://unfccc.int/topics/land-use/workstreams/redd/what-is-redd

United Nations Framework Convention on Climate Change REDD+ (UNFCCC REDD+). (2021b) *Submissions.* Available at: https://redd.unfccc.int/submissions.htmlUnited

Nations Framework Convention on Climate Change Side Events & Exhibits (UNFCCC SEORS). (2021) *Side Events & Exhibits: UN Climate Change Conference November 2021.* Available at: https://seors.unfccc.int/applications/seors/reports/events_list.html

United Nations Framework Convention on Climate Change Submissions (UNFCCC Submissions). (2021) *Submission Portal.* Available at: https://unfccc.int/process-and-meetings/parties-non-party-stakeholders/non-party-stakeholders/submissions/submission-portal

United Nations Framework Convention on Climate Change Subsidiary Body for Scientific & Technological Advice (UNFCCC STA). (2016) *Views on Issues Relating to Agriculture, Submissions from Parties & Admitted Observer Organizations, Addendum, FCCC/SBSTA/2016/MISC.1/Add.1.* Available at: https://unfccc.int/documents?search2=&search3=myanmar

United Nations Framework Convention on Climate Change Subsidiary Body for Scientific & Technological Advice (UNFCCC STA). (2019a) *SBSTA 50.* Available at: https://unfccc.int/process-and-meetings/conferences/past-conferences/bonn-climate-change-conference-june-2019/sessions/sbsta-50

United Nations Framework Convention on Climate Change Subsidiary Body for Scientific & Technological Advice (UNFCCC STA). (2019b) *The 1st Meeting of the Facilitative Working Group of the Local Communities & Indigenous Peoples Platform. Report By the Secretariat.* Available at: https://unfccc.int/documents/200102

United Nations General Assembly (UNGA). (2006) *Human Rights Council, A/Res/60/251.* Available at: www.ohchr.org/EN/HRBodies/UPR/Pages/BackgroundDocuments.aspx

United Nations General Assembly (UNGA). (2007a) *General Assembly Adopts Declaration on Rights of Indigenous Peoples; "'Major Step Forward'" Towards Human Rights for All, Says President, GA/10612, Press Release September 13, 2007.* Available at: www.un.org/press/en/2007/ga10612.doc.htm

United Nations General Assembly (UNGA). (2007b) *Institution-Building of the United Nations Human Rights Council, A/HRC/Res/5/1.* Available at: www.ohchr.org/EN/HRBodies/UPR/Pages/BackgroundDocuments.aspx

United Nations General Assembly (UNGA). (2013) *Report of the Human Rights Council on Its Seventh Organizational Meeting, A/HRC/OM/7/1.* Available at: http://ap.ohchr.org/documents/dpage_e.aspx?si=A/HRC/OM/7/1

United Nations General Assembly (UNGA). (2014) *Report of the Special Rapporteur on the Situation of Human Rights in Myanmar, Tomas Ojea Quintana, A/HRC/25/64.* Available at: www.ohchr.org/en/documents/country-reports/ahrc2564-report-special-rapporteur-situation-human-rights-myanmar-tomas

United Nations General Assembly (UNGA). (2015a) *Situation of Human Rights in Myanmar, A/HRC/RES/28/23.* Available at: http://ap.ohchr.org/documents/dpage_e.aspx?m=89

United Nations General Assembly (UNGA). (2015b) *Report of the Special Rapporteur on the Situation of Human Rights in Myanmar, Yanghee Lee, A/HRC/28/72.* Available at: http://ap.ohchr.org/documents/dpage_e.aspx?m=89

United Nations General Assembly (UNGA). (2015c) *Special Rapporteur on the Situation of Human Rights in Myanmar.* Available at: www.ohchr.org/EN/HRBodies/SP/CountriesMandates/MM/Pages/SRMyanmar.aspx

United Nations General Assembly (UNGA). (2020) *Situation of Human Rights in Myanmar, A/75/335.* Available at: https://undocs.org/A/75/335

United Nations General Assembly (UNGA). (2021) *Situation of Human Rights in Myanmar, A/76/314*. Available at: https://undocs.org/A/76/314

United Nations REDD Programme (UN REDD). (2016) *Regional Report of the Partnership Between Asia Indigenous Peoples Pact and the UN-REDD Programme in Bangladesh, Myanmar, & Vietnam*. Available at: www.unredd. net/announcements-and-news/2336-regional-report-of-the-partnership-between-asia-indigenous-peoples-pact-and-the-un-redd-programme-in-bangladesh-myanmar-and-viet-nam.html

United Nations REDD Programme (UN REDD). (2020) *Myanmar Takes Major Step in Getting REDD+ Ready*. Available at: www.un-redd.org/post/myanmar-takes-major-step-in-getting-redd-ready

United Nations REDD Programme (UN REDD). (2021) *Working Together to Save Myanmar's Forests*. Available at: http://stories.un-redd.org/working-together-to-save-myanmars-forests/

United Nations News (UN News). (2021) *Myanmar: Systematic Attack on Civilians, Rights Mechanism Reveals*, November 5, 2021. Available at: https://news.un.org/en/story/2021/11/1105082

United Nations Permanent Forum on Indigenous Issues (UNPFII). (2006) *The Concept of Indigenous Peoples, Secretariat of the Permanent Forum on Indigenous Issues, UNEP/CBD/WS-CB/LAC/1/INF/1*. Available at: www.cbd.int/doc/meetings/tk/wscblac-01/information/wscblac-01-inf-01-en.pdf

United Nations Permanent Forum on Indigenous Issues (UNPFII). (2021) *Indigenous Peoples, Indigenous Voices*. Available at: www.un.org/esa/socdev/unpfii/documents/5session_factsheet1.pdf

United Nations Security Council (UNSC). (2021) *Security Council Press Statement on Situation in Myanmar*, February 4, 2021. Available at: www.un.org/press/en/2021/sc14430.doc.htm

United Nations System Chief Executive Board (UNSCEB). (2021) *Building an Inclusive, Sustainable, & Resilient Future with Indigenous Peoples: A Call to Action*. Available at: https://unsceb.org/building-inclusive-sustainable-and-resilient-future-indigenous-peoples-call-action

Universal Declaration of Human Rights (UDHR). (1948) Available at: www.un.org/en/about-us/universal-declaration-of-human-rights

Universal Periodic Review Information Asia (UPR Info Asia). (2015) *Myanmar Review on 09 November 2015: Civil Society & Other Submissions*. Available at: www.upr-info.org/en/review/Myanmar/Session-23---November-2015/Civil-society-and-other-submissions

Universal Periodic Review Information Asia (UPR Info Asia). (2016) *Myanmar: Kicking-Off the UPR Follow-up Phase with the Burma/Myanmar UPR Forum*. Available at: www.upr-info.org/en/news/myanmar-kicking-off-the-upr-follow-up-phase-with-the-burmamyanmar-upr-forum

Urzedo, Danilo, et al. (2021) Indigenous & Local Communities Can Boost Seed Supply in the UN Decade on Ecosystem Restoration. *Ambio*. Available at: https://link.springer.com/article/10.1007/s13280-021-01593-z

Vacant, Fallow, & Virgin Land Law (VFV Law). (2012) *Vacant, Fallow, & Virgin Land Law 2012*. Available at: www.myanmar-law-library.org/law-library/laws-and-regulations/laws/myanmar-laws-1988-until-now/union-solidarity-and-development-party-laws-2012-2016/myanmar-laws-2012/pyidaungsu-hluttaw-law-no-10-2012-vacant-fallow-and-virgin-land-management-act.html

Valkonnen, Sanna & Sandra Wallenius-Korkalo. (2016) Practising Postcolonial Intersectionality: Gender, Religion, & Indigeneity in Sami Social Work. *International Social Work* 59(5): 614–626.

Van der Muur, Willem, Jacqueline Vel, Micah Fisher, & Kathryn Robinson. (2019) Changing Indigeneity Politics in Indonesia: From Revival to Projects. *The Asia Pacific Journal of Anthropology* 20(5): 379–396.

Van Dijk, Teun. (2013) Discourse, Power, & Access, in Carmen Rosa Caldas-Coulthard & Malcolm Coulthard (eds.), *Texts & Practices*. 84–106. Routledge.

Van Schendel, Willem. (2002) Geographies of Knowing, Geographies of Ignorance: Jumping Scale in Southeast Asia. *Environment & Planning D: Society & Space* 20(6): 647–668.

VFV Amendment. (2018) *Law Amending Vacant, Fallow, & Virgin Land Management Law 2018*. Available at: www.burmalibrary.org/docs25/2018-09-11-VFV-amendment-en.pdf

Vieira, Ana Carolina Alfinito & Sigrid Quack. (2016) Trajectories of Transnational Mobilization for Indigenous Rights in Brazil. *Revista de Administracao de Empresas* 56(4): 380–394.

Walbott, Linda. (2014) Indigenous Peoples in UN REDD+ Negotiations: "Importing Power" & Lobbying for Rights Through Discursive Interplay Management. *Ecology & Society* 19(1): 21–35.

Waller, Raisha. (2020) Incompatible Identities: Ethnicity, Belonging, & Exclusion in the Making of Myanmar's Democracy. *Yale University Modern Southeast Asia*. Available at: https://seasia.yale.edu/incompatible-identities-ethnicity-belonging-and-exclusion-making-myanmars-democracy

Walton, Matthew. (2013) "The Wages of Burman-ness": Ethnicity & Burman Privilege in Contemporary Myanmar. *Journal of Contemporary Asia* 43(1): 1–27.

Wani, Khursheed Ahmad & Lutfah Ariana. (2018) Impact of Climate Change on Indigenous People & Adaptive Capacity of Bajo Tribe, Indonesia. *Environmental Claims Journal* 30(4): 302–313.

Wapner, Paul. (1996) *Environmental Activism and World Civic Politics*. SUNY Press.

Wardana, Agung Made. (2012) Access to Justice for Indigenous Peoples in International Law. *Indonesian Journal of International Law* 9(2): 309–325.

Ware, Anthony & Costas Laoutides. (2018) *Myanmar's "Rohingya" Conflict*. Hurst Publishers.

Washington Post. (2021) *A Conversation with U.N. Secretary General Antonio Guterres*, February 3, 2021. Available at: www.washingtonpost.com/washington-post-live/2021/02/03/conversation-with-un-secretary-general-antnio-guterres/

Watson, Irene. (2018) *Indigenous Peoples as Subjects of International Law.* Routledge.

Welch, Cameron. (2018) *"Land Is Life, Conservancy Is Life": The San and the N≠a Jaqna Conservancy, Tsumke District West, Namibia.* Basler Afrika Bibliographen.

Wiedener, Patricia. (2009) Global Links and Environmental Flows: Oil Disputes in Ecuador. *Global Environmental Politics* 9(1): 31–57.

Wilmer, Franke & Pamela Martin. (2008) Transnational Normative Struggles and Globalization: The Case of Indigenous Peoples in Bolivia and Ecuador. *Globalizations* 5(4): 583–598.

Wilmsen, Edwin & James Denbow. (1990) Paradigmatic History of San-Speaking Peoples & Current Attempts at Revision. *Current Anthropology* 31(1990): 489–524.

Wilson, Pamela & Michelle Stewart. (2008) *Global Indigenous Media: Cultures, Poetics, and Politics.* Duke University Press.

Wolf, Richard & Frank Heidemann. (2014) Indigeneity, Performance, & the State in South Asia & Beyond. *Asian Ethnology* 73(2014): 1–12.

World Bank. (2021) *World Bank Data.* World Bank. Available at: http://data.worldbank.org/

World Justice Project. (2020) World Justice Project. Available at: http://worldjusticeproject.org/

Wright, Claire. (2014) Indigenous Mobilisation and the Law of Consultation in Peru: A Boomerang Pattern? *The International Indigenous Policy Journal* 5(4): 1–16.

Wu, Fengshi. (2005) *Doctoral Dissertation: Double-Mobilization: Transnational Advocacy Networks for China's Environment and Public Health.* University of Maryland. Available at: http://drum.lib.umd.edu/handle/1903/2970

Xanthaki, Alexandra. (2000) Indigenous Cultural Rights in International Law. *European Journal of Law Reform* 2(3): 343–368.

Xanthaki, Alexandra. (2009) *Indigenous Rights & United Nations Standards.* Cambridge University Press.

Xanthaki, Alexandra. (2014) Indigenous Rights at the United Nations: Their Impact on International Human Rights Standards. *Europa Ethnica* 71(3–4). Available at: www.researchgate.net/publication/322602600_Indigenous_rights_at_the_United_Nations_Their_impact_on_international_human_rights_standards

Xaxa, Virginius. (2016) The Global Indigenous Peoples Movement: It's Stirring in India. *Journal of Law, Property, & Society* 2(2016): 1–160.

Zentner, Emilie, et al. (2019) Ignoring Indigenous Peoples—Climate Change, Oil Development, & Indigenous Rights Clash in the Arctic National Wildlife Refuge. *Climatic Change* 155(2019): 533–544.

Zippel, Kathrin. (2004) Transnational Advocacy Networks and Policy Cycles in the European Union: The Case of Sexual Harassment. *Social Politics* 11(1): 57–85.

Index

www.ingramcontent.com/pod-product-compliance
Ingram Content Group UK Ltd.
Pitfield, Milton Keynes, MK11 3LW, UK
UKHW020416010325
455677UK00029B/914